Smart Moves

AUDREY MCCOLLUM

Audrey McCollum, M.S.W., is a board certified diplomate in clinical social work. She was educated at Vassar College and the Simmons College School of Social Work. She grew up in New York City and put aside her dream of becoming a journalist when a family member succumbed to mental illness, a tragedy which spurred her to become a psychotherapist.

She spent most of her adult life in New Haven, CT living with her husband, daughter, and son. Her professional work at the Yale University Child Study Center focused on the family in crisis. Her book, *The Chronically Ill Child: A Guide for Parents and Professionals* (Yale University Press, 1981) is a classic in its field.

After thirty-two years in New Haven, she and her family moved to New Hampshire, a move which inspired her studies of the ruptured relationships and unraveled identities that relocation can cause. Mrs. McCollum has rebuilt her private psychotherapy practice and now lives joyfully in Etna, NH.

NADIA JENSEN

Nadia Jensen, Ed.D., is an early childhood education specialist, writer, and teacher. She received her masters degree from Teachers College, Columbia University, and a doctorate in education from the University of Massachusetts–Amherst.

Dr. Jensen currently resides in Massachusetts with her husband, three children, and an assortment of pets. She and her family have moved six times in the past decade. Dr. Jensen has lived in New York, the Midwest, the South, four of the six New England states, Africa, and Scotland.

STUART A. COPANS

Dr. Stuart A. Copans is a board certified child and adolescent psychiatrist and an associate professor of psychiatry at Dartmouth Medical School. He was educated at Harvard University and Stanford Medical School and was trained in psychiatry at the University of Vermont, George Washington University, and Dartmouth Medical School.

Dr. Copans is a fellow of the American Psychiatric Association, the American Academy of Child and Adolescent Psychiatry, and the American Orthopsychiatric Association. He is also an active member of the National Cartoonist's Society.

Dr. Copans still dreams of finding his baseball card collection of 1950s Yankee and Dodgers teams, which were lost during a move in his childhood.

He and his wife Mary have raised their four children in Brattleboro, Vermont over the past twenty years and feel deeply settled there.

Smart Moves

Your Guide through the Emotional Maze of Relocation

by Audrey McCollum, M.S.W.
Nadia Jensen, Ed.D.
Stuart Copans, M.D.

SK
A Smith and Kraus Book

First published in the United States of America in 1996
by Smith and Kraus Publishers, Inc.

Brief excerpts or adaptations have been taken from *The Trauma
of Moving: Psychological Issues for Women* by Audrey T. McCollum,
©1990 Sage Publications, Inc., Newbury Park, CA. They are reprinted
by permission of Sage Publications.

Library of Congress Cataloging-in-Publication Data
McCollum, Audrey T.
Smart Moves: your guide through the emotional maze of relocation /
by Audrey McCollum, Nadia Jensen, Stuart Copans.
p. cm.
Includes bibliographical references.
ISBN 1-57525-086-1 (cloth) 1-57525-079-9 (paper)
1. Life change events. 2. Stress (Psychology) 3. Relocation (Housing)–
Psychological aspects. I. Jensen, Nadia. II. Copans, Stuart. III. Title.
BF637.L53M38   1996
155.9'4–dc20   96-24012
CIP

Acknowledgments

We thank Gail Baker and Mardrey Swenson, who have moved several times with their husbands and children, for reading portions of our manuscript. Their comments were thought-provoking and constructive.

We thank all those other movers who shared their personal stories with frankness and trust. In order to protect their privacy, we have assigned them fictitious names, occupations, and geographic locations.

Lisa Leslie-Henderson, also a mover, contributed energy, enthusiasm, and expertise in helping us develop a marketing plan.

Our own three families have buoyed our work with their keen interest, warm encouragement, and practical help. Bob McCollum has gone far beyond the extra mile in contributing his time, energy, resources, and wisdom to the project, and in soothing the senior author whenever her computer went berserk.

Finally, we thank our publishers—Marisa Smith, Eric Kraus, and their production director, Julia Hill. Because of their responsiveness, flexibility, and creativity, we have had a unique experience of collaboration in bringing this work to fruition.

Dedication

To Bob, Richard, and Mary—our beloved partners.

CONTENTS

INTRODUCTION

All the Ways This Book Will Help

There are surges of change in the USA each year as more than forty million people relocate their homes. Every aspect of those lives can be affected.

The sunny side of moving is well known. For some, it's the path to survival. For many, it's a quest for improvement—finer housing, better jobs, more education, different lifestyles, new relationships, fresh purpose in life.

The shadow side of moving has been unrecognized. Yet no matter how much a move is wanted, no matter how successful it may turn out to be, most movers experience grinding stresses that take a physical and emotional toll.

Our purpose in writing this book is to help you turn stress into strength. The more clearly you understand the challenges you face and the reactions you can expect in yourself and your loved ones, the more effectively you'll meet those challenges. Even an unwanted move can become successful.

This may be your initial move or one of many. Yet each move is a "first" since you're at a different age and a different life phase than before. This time you may be with or without a parent or partner, with or without children, or with children at different stages of development. The strategies you used before may help you again, but you'll need new ones too.

Our book is intended for three groups of people: those of you who are considering a "some day" move, those of you facing an immediate move, and those who have recently moved. We guide you through the complexities of relocation, using real-life stories as signposts along the way.

Moving doesn't start with packing boxes. It begins when the idea first comes to mind. In Section One, we challenge those of you considering a move to explore the full range of your reasons, questioning whether moving will really solve your problem, and considering solutions in addition to relocation. We nudge you to think about all the sources of happiness and discouragement in your present lives. We spur you to consider the emotional and social tasks that you and your loved ones face in moving. We suggest ways of learning about "maybe" places. We show you how to make a win-win decision that takes into account the needs of everyone in the family.

When you've finished reading this section, you may decide that moving would be unwise at this time. But even if you decide against a geographic move, you will have made a positive psychological move. That is, you will have seen your life (and the lives of your loved ones) through a fresh lens—clarifying your satisfactions and frustrations, your dreams and disappointments, your capabilities and vulnerabilities, and identifying your priorities. It was Plato who sagely declared, "An unexamined life is scarcely worth living."

If you know for certain that you are going to move, you may be tempted to skip over this first section of the book. We urge you not to, and here's why. First of all, although you can surely identify one paramount reason for moving, you may have other needs you've been ignoring. For example, perhaps you've finally been offered a new job after months of desperate searching. You've accepted the job, and that's why you're moving. But there are other choices to be made. Are you also hoping to live in a neighborhood where real estate costs are lower so you can finally buy a house? Or an area that's close to the beach? It's important to know as much as possible about your aims as you plan where and how to live in a new community.

Second, you may be moving with a spouse, partner, parent, or children. Their reasons for wanting to move may be quite different from yours. Your partner may be dreaming of going back to school, starting a home-based consulting firm, or taking early retirement. S/he may see your move as the perfect opportunity. Or your loved ones may be horrified at the prospect of relocation. Their needs and hopes should be taken into account as you decide how to reconstruct your lives. Section One will help.

For those whose decision is "let's go," Section Two offers guidelines for preparing all family members for the move: handling the pain of good-byes; planning continuities in your lives; arranging to be welcomed into the new community; developing strategies to buffer the tumult of moving day. Your employer's relocation office, your library, realtor, or van line can supply useful information about the practicalities–financing your move, packing your household goods, finding new housing. Our aims are to help you understand the powerful emotions that may be stirred up, and to find ways to preserve your sense of safety and competence, as well as your self-esteem. And we suggest how you can effectively shepherd your children through the unsettled times.

In Section Three, we look closely at the challenge of connecting with new people and places. We explore the feelings you and your children are likely to have (especially those that may take you by surprise) and the effects they can have on your love relationships. We offer ideas about coping with those feelings. After that, we suggest strategies to help you and your loved ones build meaningful new lives. We suggest ways to develop new roles and relationships, even as you preserve the parts of your lives that brought fulfillment in the past.

There are probably people in your present community who care about you a lot and want your move to be successful. This book will help them as they search for ways to help you. It can also help people in your new community find ways to make you feel at home.

At the end of each chapter, you'll find exercises designed for every member of the immediate family, children and adults. You may want to write your responses into this book, or copy the headings into a notebook that becomes your journal. Or you may simply want to use them to clarify your thoughts without writing.

Do the exercises on your own at first, then compare your responses with those of other family members. Using them can help each of you apply our ideas to your individual life. They can increase your understanding of each other's thoughts and feelings, and serve as guidelines for discussions about the move. They can help draw you together as you face a significant turning point in your lives.

NOTE: From this point on, we'll use the word "partner" to designate the person with whom you've formed an intimate relationship. Although many among you are husbands or wives, there are also many who are unmarried but in a committed love relationship. The book is for you, too, as well as widows, widowers, divorcees, and other singles who aren't in an intimate relationship.

Introduction Exercise

YOUR MOVING HISTORY

Some of you have fascinating tales to tell about your moves in childhood, adolescence, and adulthood. Your stories may be filled with sadness as well as joy and dreams-come-true, often all in one story. On the other hand, some of you who have moved rarely or never can tell poignant stories of having a beloved friend or family member move away.

Before you go further in our book, consider reviewing your own moving history. It doesn't matter if you've moved a lot, a little, or not at all—your memories are likely to have a powerful influence over your approach to the move you're now considering, the move you've decided to make, or the move you've just made.

If you are moving with a partner, child, or parent, we encourage you to tell each other what you remember and what you have learned from your own histories.

NOTE TO PARENTS: This exercise is especially useful to work on with your children, even if you're only thinking about moving across town. For example, your fourteen year old will probably be relieved to hear that you had the same worries about going to a new high school that s/he has been having. Or, if you have never moved, you can support your child by being honest: "I never moved as a kid, and I'm new at being new, too." The most important message to convey is that you will help your children in their transitions to a new home, new neighborhood, and new school.

SECTION ONE

To Move or Not to Move?

CHAPTER 1

There's a Move on Your Mind

There's a variety of reasons why you may have the urge to move, reasons connected with jobs, finances, education, environment, health, emotional states, and personal relationships. Moving can certainly lead to positive life changes. Yet dreams don't always come true. A move may not provide what you need, especially if you're vague about your aims.

In this chapter we focus on clarifying your motives. We give examples of people who moved for different reasons. Those vignettes may give you fresh ideas about how to think about relocation. The exercises at the end of the chapter encourage you take a full inventory of the reasons why there's a move on your mind. You may discover motives you didn't know you had.

OCCUPATIONAL MOTIVES

JOBS! JOBS! JOBS! Those have always comprised an urgent reason for moving. In many realms of work, basic security as well as advancement have been intertwined with geographic mobility. Now, as global and national economies are changing, large numbers of organizations are relocating facilities, restructuring operations, and "downsizing" both blue and white collar staffs.

It can be exciting but deeply unsettling to be told that your place in the firm depends on your willingness to relocate, and that your decision must be made within days or even hours. It may seem ludicrous to consider asking yourself or your partner why you want to move when your job or your promotion hinges on it. Yet this is actually a fine time to take stock of your aims.

You may want to develop new skills. You may want to apply your talents to new challenges. You may want more knowledgeable supervisors, more responsibility, or more independence. You may want to join a growing trend and work out of your home with computer, modem, and fax.

At the threshold of change, why not explore those possibilities with your employer? Why not negotiate a new way of using your skills? If relocation seems essential, your clarity of purpose can get you off to a satisfying start in the new location. Or you may decide that it's time to search for a different job.

It is shattering to be downsized—a new euphemism for fired. Even if you have confidence in your knowledge and skills and a solid record of achievement, any lurking self-doubt will come out of hiding if the company doesn't want you. "Why me?" you'll wonder as you wrestle with anxiety, anger, and sadness.

If you have been fired, or your firm is closing down, your employer may refer you to an outplacement counselor who will involve you in a survey of your skills and help you locate new opportunities. That also may not happen. Try then to remind yourself that adversity can be turned into opportunity. Use Chapters 1 and 2 of this book to learn more about yourself and broaden the range of your choices.

RANDY

Randy was a thirty-nine-year-old professor of economics when the small private college where he taught closed down for financial reasons. His first thought was to search the nation for openings in other colleges. Yet Randy, his wife Phyllis, and their school-age children felt happily settled in their town. So after much self-questioning and many family discussions, Randy's courageous choice was to draw on his knowledge of economics and become an independent entrepreneur. He was successful, but he still cherishes the hope that when the children are grown, he and Phyllis will build a life elsewhere so that he can resume the teaching he loves. Meanwhile, though, he's developed capabilities he wasn't sure he had. He's made a psychological move rather than a geographic one.

If you are transferred or fired or your workplace collapses, the idea of moving is imposed on you from outside. But it may be the other way around. You may want to move as a way of escaping job pressures.

MARIAN

Marian, a forty-one-year-old nurse midwife whose help was sought around the clock, dealt with mounting exhaustion by taking time out. Since, in her community, she would have been cajoled to take "just one more case," she decided to make a temporary move—a year in another state to tackle different challenges and gain a fresh perspective on her life. In the new milieu she used her professional skills in other ways. Rather than being a nurse clinician, she became a consultant on women's health care needs. Her temporary relocation was so effective that it led to a permanent change.

Marian used relocation as an opportunity to rethink her aims. Others let that chance slip by.

ZEKE

Zeke, a fifty-three-year-old psychologist, also moved to escape pressure in his work. He had a successful private practice in a New England college town—so successful that evening and week-end hours were absorbed into his professional schedule. As his energy flagged, it felt like time to make a fresh start in another place. Zeke moved to a carefully chosen college town in the south. It had many of the features he would have enjoyed in New England if he had taken the time. Did Zeke enjoy them in the south? He didn't find out. Within two years, he had allowed his psychotherapy practice to consume him as it had before.

Before he decided on an external move, Zeke would have been wise to make some internal moves—to look inside himself and learn why he had such difficulty saying "I'm sorry I can't take you into therapy, but I can give you the name of a capable colleague."

If your work demands high energy and emotional responsiveness, as Zeke's and Marian's did, you may become drained by its intensity. Or if you've allowed the pace of work as an investment banker to crowd out other realms of your life— love relationships, vacations, even tennis games, moving to "get away from the rat race" may feel urgent. A new beginning in a different place can be a constructive solution to burnout, but only if you can take charge of the inner needs that led you to become overwhelmed where you live now.

PSYCHOLOGICAL MOTIVES

Your problem may not be a too-full life, but an empty one— or the fear of it.

SUSAN

"I'm always searching for new experiences. I can't just read National Geographic, I have to actually be in those places," Susan, a twenty-seven-year-old frequent mover explained. "I feel as though I'm on a river, rushing through the rapids. But when I come to calmer waters, I won't simply float— I'll sink into lethargy and hopelessness." Soon after each move, the dread of sinking into that bleak state would overtake her again. Susan was a psychological gypsy, trying to fend off depression through restless mobility. Counseling proved more helpful for her than frantic moves.

Although you may not experience states as extreme as Susan's, your life may seem empty at times. You may feel a loss of zest in your work, your play, your friendships, your love relationships. Days may drag on, drab and monotonous. It's easy to imagine that living in a new place would rekindle your usual enthusiasm. That can indeed happen. New places, people, and challenges can rev you up. But before you rupture all your connections, try to be reasonably sure that the source of the drabness is outside yourself, and not within.

If you feel occasionally bored, new experiences can help. Maybe a wind surfing club, a painting class, a language course, a political campaign, or volunteering in a hospital will give you a lift and restore your sense of making a difference in the world. If you can't find such challenges where you now are, you may need to move to find them.

But if every sphere of your life has lost its zest, your boredom may reflect a psychological depression which you would carry with you through a move, and which moving could even intensify. It's wise to seek professional guidance before you decide to relocate.

TROUBLED LOVE RELATIONSHIPS

You may have the urge to move away from a troubled love relationship. If your partner is physically abusive, leaving may save your life. But if the abuse is emotional—your partner is self-absorbed, critical, disdainful, for example—there is a choice. You may want distance in order to experience your own needs, rights, wishes, competencies apart from his or hers. Physical separation may clarify your sense of self, but will it strengthen your capacity to communicate constructively with your partner? You may need to work on that while you live together, perhaps with the help of a couples' therapist.

Your faltering relationship may or may not be strengthened, so the question of moving may surge up again. The breakdown of a marriage is a common reason for relocation. Beyond leaving the shared home, you may want to leave the community in which the relationship failed, distancing from the reminders of your earlier happiness, your later misery. But before you decide, remember that the emotions those reminders stir up may not stay behind. If you feel guilty or ashamed because the relationship failed, those feelings may follow you through the move. They may become even more troublesome because you must struggle through them without the support of close friends and colleagues.

RETIREMENT

GOLF! GOLF! GOLF! That's an enticing image for many. Or 329 sunny days each year. As you approach retirement, those images may pull you towards a move. Thousands of Americans do retire to the "sunshine states." But some return to where they came from because the move hasn't met their needs.

Your daydreams about how to enjoy your well-earned leisure deserve serious attention (in Chapter 4, we discuss many things to consider as you search for a community to retire in). An immediate question, though, is whether it's wise to move and retire at the same time. Your identity may be primarily embedded in your career—common for men and growing numbers of women. How will it feel to set that aside while you're giving up all your other roles and attachments in your present community? It may be wiser to do it in stages. Be comfortable first with the new identity—golf player rather than editor—while you're still nurtured by your friends and community, and then move later.

Health problems, aging, or aloneness may have reduced your capacity to manage your household. But consider new ways of coping before undertaking a major disruption, especially in this life stage when continuities can be crucial.

LAURA

Laura moved out of her beloved family house in her eightieth year, feeling physically unable to maintain it. Her sadness at the loss of this home—permeated with memories of family life and gatherings of friends—was profound and prolonged. But Laura lived near a university. Might there have been students who would have happily accepted comfortable housing in exchange for housekeeping and grounds keeping chores? Wouldn't a one year trial have been worthwhile?

If Laura had scanned her life, considering the people, places, and roles that gave it special meaning, she might have delayed her move. In the next chapter, we encourage you to scan your own.

Chapter 1 Exercises

These exercises can help you clarify your own reasons for considering a move. If you have a partner, we encourage each of you to complete them on your own, and then show them to each other (you may want to use a simple notebook to jot down your thoughts).

EXERCISE A

We've prepared an inventory of reasons for considering a move. Think about the questions we've asked. Note the items that most closely reflect what you've been thinking about or feeling. After each set of reasons there are four open-ended statements to help you crystallize your thoughts.

1. Question: Are you thinking about a move because of special needs and interests related to EMPLOYMENT and INCOME?
  · I have to move to find a job.
  · I have to move to advance in my field.
  · I've dreamed of working in a different field.
  · I'd like more opportunities in my job (e.g. more independence, more responsibility, better supervision etc.).
  · I need a less demanding job.
  · I may want to relocate after I retire.
  · I'd like a higher salary.
  · I'd like to live in a more affordable home/community.
  · I'd like to live in a more upscale area.

Now try to complete the following statements.
  My needs/hopes concerning EMPLOYMENT and INCOME include

  _____

  _____

  My partner's needs/hopes concerning EMPLOYMENT/ INCOME include

  _____

  _____

  Moving would help me meet these needs by

  _____

  _____

If I decide to stay here, I could meet these needs by

_____

_____

2. Question: Are you thinking about a move because of special needs and interests related to EDUCATION?

- · I'd like to attend school/college/university in another area.
- · My professional education requires relocation.
- · The kind of school I want my children to attend is in another community.
- · My children need special educational services that exist in another community.

Now try to complete the following statements.

My needs/hopes concerning EDUCATION include

_____

_____

My partner's needs/hopes concerning education include

_____

_____

Moving would help me meet these needs by

_____

_____

If I stay here, I could meet these needs by

_____

_____

3. Question: Are you thinking about a move because of special needs and interests related to your ENVIRONMENT?

· I'd like to move away from environmental hazards.
· I'd like to live in a different climate.

Now try to complete the following statements.

My needs/hopes concerning ENVIRONMENT include

_____

_____

My partner's needs/hopes concerning ENVIRONMENT include

_____

_____

Moving would help me meet these needs by

_____

_____

If I stay here I could meet these needs by

_____

_____

4. Question: Are you thinking about a move because of some of your RELATIONSHIPS?

· I'm ready to move away from my birth family.
· I'm in a love relationship and want to live with or near my partner.
· I'd like a separation from my partner.
· I'm ending my love relationship, and want to move away from my partner.
· I'd like to get away from a difficult relationship with a friend, family member, colleague, neighbor.

Now try to complete the following statements.

My needs/hopes concerning RELATIONSHIPS include

_____

_____

My partner's needs/hopes concerning RELATIONSHIPS include

_____

_____

Moving would help me meet these needs by

_____

_____

If I stay here I could meet these needs by

_____

_____

5. Question: Are you considering a move because of EMOTIONAL NEEDS?

- I'm bored and wonder if moving would make my life more interesting.
- I'm lonely and searching for new companions and friends.
- I'm depressed and think a change of scene might help.
- I'm afraid of isolation; I don't want to be alone if I need help.
- I'm trying to get away from painful memories.

Now try to complete the following statements.

Right now, my EMOTIONAL NEEDS include

_____

_____

Right now, my partner's EMOTIONAL NEEDS include

_____

_____

Moving could help me meet these needs by

_____

_____

If I stay here I could meet these needs by

_____

_____

EXERCISE B

Now, as you think about changing your life, let your imagination soar...

1. Imagine that you have just won the lottery. On the first of each month for the next twenty-five years you will receive a check for $20,000.

How would your life change?

_____

_____

Would you move?

_____

Where would you move to?

_____

Why would you move there?

_____

_____

2. Imagine that, for reasons of safety, you and your family had to leave your community for at least twenty-five years.

What would you miss most?

_____

_____

Where would you go?

_____

_____

What would you do?

_____

_____

3. Imagine that, for reasons of safety, you had to keep on living in your community for at least twenty-five years.

How would this situation change your life?

_____

_____

What would you do to make the situation better?

_____

_____

Would you remain in your current home? Why?

_____

_____

CHAPTER 2

Scan Your Life:
Where You've Been, Where You Are,
Where You Want to Go

The momentum of your daily life rarely allows for contemplation. Weeks, months, years speed by and you often feel caught up by forces you hardly understand, shaped by needs you barely recognize, energized by aims that you've not consciously chosen.

The prospect of moving provides a special opportunity. It can spur you to take a fresh look, a deep look, and a wide-ranging look at your life.

Clarifying why you're considering a move is an important start, but you need to go further. Since a move may affect every aspect of your life, you need to embark on a journey of self-discovery. You need to ask yourself, "Who am I, and who do I want to become?"

For men and women, these questions can be awkward in different ways. Many women find it difficult to distinguish the "I" from the "We." From early in life, they've been encouraged to think of themselves as connected with others—being cared for by others and/or giving care to others. The psychological boundaries between the self and the other may feel quite fluid. In love relationships and close friendships, a woman has moments of merging, feeling at one with the other. There can be an unspoken communion of thought and emotion.

Because of these fluid boundaries between self and other, it is difficult for many women to distinguish their needs and dreams from those of their intimates. Further, although a man who declares "I am" or "I want" is seen as decisive and self-confident, a woman who does that may be labeled self-centered. She may think of herself that way too.

Since we value the "I" of individuality and independence in men, the personhood of a man should be easier to define. Yet men are encouraged to look outward rather than inward, toward action rather than introspection. And they are encouraged to center on thoughts rather than feelings. A man is rarely encouraged to know his whole being.

With our children, we focus on behavior: "What have you done, what are you doing, what are you going to do?" We ask less often, "What are you thinking, what are you feeling, what are you imagining?"

Yet every prospective mover—man, woman, and older child—should explore this question: "Who am I as an individual, deeply connected with my loved ones but also distinct?" The answers will help you understand what you need, individually and as a family, to feel secure, effective, significant, loving, and loved. The risks and benefits of a move should be measured against that understanding. If you do decide to move, or if you have to move, you will know what to search for in a new community to fulfill your needs, hopes and dreams.

Your selfhood is composed of many strands. The question, "Who am I?" includes other questions: What is my work? How do I renew myself? What places are important to me? What people are important to me?

WHAT IS YOUR WORK?

You may think of work as an occupation carried out for pay, usually outside of the home. That work, the source of your livelihood, is probably essential. But other realms of work are important too in binding together families and communities. So we'll define work as any investment of time and energy toward fulfilling a serious goal. It includes schoolwork, homemaking, and voluntary work as well as a paid occupation.

Work often generates income, but it also fulfills psychological needs. Work gives you an identity. It allows you to feel effective, using your abilities to make a difference in the world. Work brings appreciation of your competence and your specialness. For men, women, and older children, work is a wellspring of self-esteem.

"What are *all* of my realms of work?" you need to ask yourself in doing your Lifescan. Are you a Little League coach as well as an engineer? A political organizer as well as a homemaker? A hospital volunteer as well as a realtor? All these roles give you an identity in the eyes of others, and contribute to your inner sense of self: "This is who I am."

What are your goals in the work you do? What work has the highest priority? What work makes you feel useful and effective? Who and what validates your work—is it the trusting smile of the sick child you soothe in the hospital, the election of your political candidate, or the realtor-of-the-year award? Could your lines of work be developed elsewhere?

Few people work in isolation. So your Lifescan should include these questions, "Who are my colleagues? What part do they play in encouraging my work, affirming its importance, sharing my problems, and finding solutions? How would it feel to do my work without them?"

Homemakers, especially women, too readily subscribe to the myth that their work is transportable, easily carried from Philadelphia to Duluth. Do you? Do you believe that you can be a wife and mother anywhere? In some respects you can. You can listen sympathetically to your partner's problems anywhere. You can hug your crying child anywhere. You can cook a meal and do the laundry almost anywhere. But think about the interruptions, repetitions, frustrations, worries, and lonely moments that are inevitable in any homemaker's life. What helps you tolerate those? Think about the network you've created to support your work—other parents to share problems and solutions with, play groups for your children, a daycare center and a roster of babysitters, a trusting relationship with the children's doctor and teachers. And what about the plumber who'll be there fast when the sink overflows, or the fishmonger who'll save the freshest piece of salmon for your family?

How readily could those special people be replaced? Or do you need to move to find such people because you can't find them where you are?

HOW DO YOU RENEW YOURSELF?

Few people can sustain a commitment to effective work and successful love relationships without interludes for physical, emotional, intellectual and spiritual renewal. How do you seek your renewal?

HOW DO YOU PLAY?

Although you can be playful in your work, and you may work hard at your play, most people think of the realms as separate. Play may seem less important than work. It's not. Play can replenish you in myriad necessary ways.

As you do a Lifescan, ask yourself these questions: "How do I play? Do I enjoy talking politics in a city cafe? Do I like to lose myself in the image-laden world of theatres, art galleries, and concerts? Do I want to test myself in tennis matches? Would I rather watch the Red Sox struggle? Does sewing a new dress replenish me, or gathering friends for a barbecue, or gliding through the water in a kayak?"

"Who are my playmates? Could my scuba buddy, my string quartet, my bridge club be readily replaced if I moved?"

"Where do I play? Do I depend on special facilities—a gym, a pool, a running track, a woodworking shop or pottery kiln? Can they be found elsewhere? Or do I need facilities in a different place in order to live out a dream?"

"Among the identities I forge through my play—clarinetist, golfer, dressmaker, third baseman—which feel most important?"

YOUR SPIRITUAL LIFE

For some, spirituality means sensing the pulse of creation. It means sitting on an ocean beach, watching, hearing, smelling, tasting the curling, pounding surf. It means walking through an ancient forest, noticing the mosses, the ferns, the new life on a decaying log. It means floating across a coral reef marveling at the palette of colors and intricate forms.

For some, spirituality means a direct communion with God through prayer, perhaps in a simple Quaker meeting house.

For some, spirituality means the ancient ritual acts, words, and music carried out in a synagogue or a Catholic church.

How do you make your connection with the creator or God that you believe in? How do you renew your awareness of meaning in your life?

WHAT PLACES ARE SPECIAL IN YOUR LIFE?

YOUR HOME

The place you live in—whether it's a tiny apartment or a mansion— may feel like home. Or it may not. What do you really mean by home?

Home may be a shelter that enfolds you and feels cozy, strong, and warm. It may be a safe place where you feel both protected and competent. It may be a familiar place that you know your way around, perhaps even in the dark.

Home is a place where you belong. It's a place where you can be yourself and express yourself.

Think about your relationship to your home, asking yourself, "In what ways is my personhood anchored in my home? Do the colors of the walls, the patterns of the fabrics, the arrangement of the furniture, the placement of mementos express my taste, ideas, emotions, daydreams?"

"How does my home shape my relations to others? Does it give me and my loved ones the closeness we want or the distance and privacy we need? Is it a gathering place for neighbors or friends? Is it the playground for my children's friends?"

"Is my home a history book, filled with personal memories and memories of family and friends? Could that history be carried to another place?"

"Am I most strongly attached to the structure of my home, the arrangement of the rooms, the orientation to the sun, the views out of the windows? Which are the elements in my home that I truly love? Which elements do I long for but don't yet have? Which among them could be created, or recreated, in another dwelling?"

Home also extends outside the dwelling, and it's easy to forget the importance of your neighborhood. So ask yourself these questions:

"Do I need exposure to the sights and sounds of neighbors to feel safely connected, or a shield of privacy to feel safely protected?"

"Do I want a mixture of races and ethnic traditions to enrich my daily life? Or do I feel most secure among neighbors who share my own roots and traditions—people whose color is the same as mine, whose accents sound the same, people who celebrate the same holidays I celebrate?"

"Do I need urban bustle to keep me tuned up? Or do I need rural calm to keep me soothed?"

"How do I and my family use the space around our home? Is there an apple tree begging to be climbed? Do my small ones ride tricycles up and down the sidewalk? Is there an empty lot or a dead-end street nearby for a pick-up soccer game? A field for a romp with our dog?"

"Do I have a garden where I can be involved in the renewal of life, watching the first daffodil shoots emerge in the spring, harvesting the tiniest zucchinis at summer's height?"

OTHER SPECIAL PLACES

Your life is filled with special places, although you may never have realized how much they mean. There are places you work and places you play, places you mingle, places you feast. There are places you go to feel at peace and dream—places that have private meanings.

A firehouse was the special place for eight-year-old Jason. After school, his feet just took him there. There was a friendly dalmatian, the thrill of the siren and the firefighters leaping aboard their gleaming trucks. But most important, there was hanging out between the calls—hanging out with some kindly guys who joked and spun tales about their boyhood, and asked Jason about his own. Over time, those guys seemed like big brothers or uncles or even fathers for a boy whose true father was a successful banker who rarely had time for his son.

Marcia's special place provided tranquil solitude. When this fifteen year old felt on the brink of "losing it" because of her stormy battles with her mother, she retreated to an abandoned fire tower on a hill above her town. The vista of ancient hills and a meandering river below was calming, and her turmoil would slowly subside.

Your special places can meet many different needs. While you're identifying them, remind yourself how you get there. Transportation can be the web that connects the myriad segments of your life. Do you safely walk or bike? Rely on the subway or bus? Is driving everywhere a must, and is that what you really want?

WHAT PEOPLE ARE SPECIAL IN YOUR LIFE?

Most of the realms of your work, play, spiritual life and health, involve relationships with other people. A move may involve a multitude of separations. For some movers, the rupture of personal relationships causes intense pain—we'll say more about that in later chapters. On the other hand, you may be considering a move because you need relationships that you don't now have. Think now about all your relationships, and their meanings in your life.

WHO ARE YOUR FRIENDS?

We live in a society in which independence and separation are highly valued, rather than interdependence and connection. So the importance of close friendship is often overlooked, especially when people are considering a move. In this realm, men and women seem to differ.

Women define close friendship in these ways. There is mutuality—shared values, interests, and experiences—giving rise to an empathic bond that allows each to understand the other's thoughts and feelings. There is spontaneity—close friends can turn to each other on the spur of the moment and depend on each other's responsiveness. Close friendship is authentic—the mutual concern is genuine. There is trust—each friend feels safe in exposing her private self to the other, confident that even her flaws will be accepted. There is reciprocity—each friend is both active and passive, giving and taking, nurturing and nourished. Each partner in a friendship feels understood, cared about, valued, and supported.

Some women are aware of how much those friendships matter. Even then, their specialness can be unnoticed. Another myth about moving can cloud women's thoughts—the myth that close friends are easily replaced.

Men seem less disposed towards confiding their private thoughts, feelings, and daydreams to buddies, although some do turn to wives and lovers in the ways that women turn to intimate women friends. But men do form deep bonds as they share experiences. For Hank, it was working with his male partner on a town rescue squad that deepened the bonds. For William, it was the yearly backwoods fishing trip with three buddies that fostered the attachment. Yet men rarely articulate the meaning those bonds have in their lives. Even more rarely do they factor them into a decision about relocation.

For children, friends have increasing importance as the years go by. They play a special part in the development of gender identity (the sense of being masculine or being feminine) and the growth of independence.

A boy is expected to become independent from his parents, especially his mother. But he needs a sense of belonging, and his father—if he has one—may not be very available. So he relies on "the guys." The support of "the guys" helps a boy quell his lingering wishes for closeness to his mom. The guys support each other to suppress whatever feels babyish or sissyish in themselves and each other. They join to buttress their masculinity by despising girls and showing their prowess on the playing fields. They share their interest in their developing sexuality.

There's less pressure on girls to become independent from their mothers, but they still have to tolerate increasing amounts of separation as daycare or school days grow longer and after-school activities more numerous. So they turn to friends too—less likely a gang, more likely one or two intimates with whom they share their dilemmas about becoming women.

For both boys and girls, affectionate friendships form a bridge between the early intense attachments to parents and later commitment to a love partner. And their developing sense of self is strengthened as they try out their own values, behavior, and ideas on others, and are exposed to other children's ways of being.

If you are considering a move, it's important to help your child or teenager identify other youngsters s/he cares about—classmates, teammates, neighborhood gangs, kids from the church, country club, or recreation center, co-workers at after school jobs. And encourage him or her to think about special grown-ups. You'd be likely to think of teachers, coaches, and camp counselors. But would you think of people like the fire-fighters who played such an important role in Jason's young life?

WHAT ABOUT YOUR FAMILY?

Up to this point, your Lifescan has focused on the characteristics and needs of individuals. The aims and needs of your marriage or love partnership, and of your family as a whole need attention too.

For couples, the prospect of a move offers a special opportunity to look together at your individual lives, and to look at your shared life too. It is a time to explore together your hopes and fears, capabilities and limits, dreams and realities. It's a time to consider together how a move might shape your lives as individuals and as a melded twosome.

For example, the highest proportion of American movers are between twenty–thirty-four years of age. This is the time of life when most men and women are intensely involved in developing love relationships and starting new families, as well as building the foundations of their careers. If you're among them, you're probably taxed to the utmost.

Our culture of independence and mobility has led to the dispersion of kinfolk across the land. "Nuclear" families—husband, wife, and children—tend to be overburdened in today's fragmented society, and single-parent or same-sex parent families even more so. Every family member seems to need a "goodwife"—that is, a soothing, loving, available presence dedicated to the happiness of the family. Men and children need them, and sometimes have them. Women need them, too.

When she was thirty-seven, Patricia placed an ad in the Help Wanted section of her newspaper: "Married female business executive with children needs a wife." There were seventeen replies within two days. They came from women who immediately understood her need for a person to create order, calm, and welcoming warmth in her house, and turn it into a haven for the family. The "goodwife" Patricia chose came into her home every day. But there can be others outside the home who play that role as well.

Who are the "goodwives" for the members of your family? Are there familiar, trustworthy, concerned, and comforting neighbors, colleagues, clergy, teachers, or health professionals available to you now? Do you have family-to-family friendships that take the place of biological kin? How might your family be affected if you lost those sources of comfort and support?

Not all biological kin live far apart. What role do parents, aunts, uncles, brothers, sisters, and adult children play in your lives? What part do you play in theirs? If you are still living close to each other, do they rejoice with you in your successes and comfort you in your failures? Do they give advice when you want it, and cheerfully encourage when you don't? Do they offer companionship, time, muscle, and money? Do you do those things for them?

Would it be a relief or a sorrow to live further apart? If you moved away, could you preserve a good relationship by letter or phone, without hugs and gestures and reading each other's faces? Could you still gather at the most special times—birthdays, Thanksgiving, Christmas, Passover? How might it feel if you couldn't?

If you're an introspective person, scanning across the many realms of your life may seem intriguing and easy. You might do it while you stroll along a beach, soak in a long, hot, tub, or shell the peas for dinner. But to some of you, it may sound tedious— you'd rather be doing than reflecting. Our worksheets may capture your interest.

To others, a Lifescan may seem like a pointless effort, especially if you feel forced to move. But even if a move seems necessary, you may have choices about where to go. And if not that, you will have choices about how to reconstruct your life. Heedlessly, many movers make unfortunate choices for themselves. Needlessly, they suffer as a result.

So we urge you to give it a try. Encourage a family member or a friend to do a Lifescan with you. Learning more about yourselves and each other will enhance your capacity to make wise choices in every realm of your life, and it may draw you closer together.

Chapter 2 Exercises

You've been reading about some of the places, things, people, and events that have special meanings in peoples' lives. In the exercises for this chapter you can complete your own Lifescan as you look carefully at the WHO, WHAT, and WHERE(s) you have come to value. You, your partner and your older children may want to complete Lifescans separately, and then look at them together. You may learn a lot of new things about each other.

EXERCISE A

As I think about moving, I realize that:

I need

_____

_____

I want

_____

_____

I dream about

_____

_____

I'm sometimes afraid of

_____

_____

My "goodwife" (see p.25) is/can be

_____ (name of person/s)

I can be a "goodwife" for

_____ (name of person/s)

EXERCISE B

Here we've included a list of some things, people, places, events that are significant in many people's lives. In order to complete your "Lifescan," we suggest the following steps:

FIRST: Read through the entire list below.

THEN: Without spending too much time on each item, put a check next to anything on the list that you consider important.

AGAIN: Look at each item you have checked and ask yourself:

· In what ways does this person, place, etc. make me feel understood, supported, cared about, and valued?

· How would it feel to live without this person or place?

· How readily could I replace this person or place if I move?

· If I move, how easily could I find those special persons, places, etc. that are currently missing from my life?

LIFESCAN ITEMS

Paid job_____

Neighborhood/Community_____

Transportation services____

Shops and stores____

Volunteer work_____

Colleagues_____

Friends_____

Family members_____

Ethnic diversity____

Arts/entertainment programs_____

Religious organizations____

Health care providers_____

Educational programs (adults'/children's)____

Recreational areas/centers_____

Climate_____

Emergency/rescue services____

Personal/family safety___
Environment_____
Repair services____
Senior citizen's center_____
Your home: Inside____Outside____
Special Celebrations____

Other Items? List below.

_____

_____

EXERCISE C

List the people (outside your household) you talk to in person every day.

_____	_____	_____
_____	_____	_____
_____	_____	_____
_____	_____	_____

List the people (outside your household) you talk to in person every week.

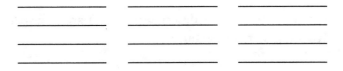

_____	_____	_____
_____	_____	_____
_____	_____	_____
_____	_____	_____

List the people (outside your household) you talk to in person every month.

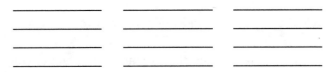

_____	_____	_____
_____	_____	_____
_____	_____	_____
_____	_____	_____

List the people you talk to on the phone every day.

_____   _____   _____
_____   _____   _____
_____   _____   _____
_____   _____   _____

List the people you talk to on the phone every week.

_____   _____   _____
_____   _____   _____
_____   _____   _____
_____   _____   _____

List the people you would miss seeing and/or talking to.

_____   _____   _____
_____   _____   _____
_____   _____   _____
_____   _____   _____

List the people you would be relieved not to see or talk to.

_____   _____   _____
_____   _____   _____
_____   _____   _____
_____   _____   _____

List twelve nouns that describe who you are (e.g. parent, lawyer, golfer, and so on).

_____   _____   _____
_____   _____   _____
_____   _____   _____
_____   _____   _____

Circle the five that are most important to you.

List the three belongings that are most important to you.

_____   _____   _____

What makes each one important?

_____

_____

_____

List your six favorite places.

_____   _____   _____

_____   _____   _____

What is special about each place?

_____

_____

_____

_____

_____

_____

List the six friends who are most important to you.

_____   _____   _____

_____   _____   _____

What makes each friend important?

_____

_____

_____

_____

_____

_____

CHAPTER 3

Never Underestimate the Power of Your Move

"A move can be really high stress even when you want to do it," declared Nina, a recent mover. "You don't anticipate that, so your reactions are confusing and frightening. You expected to feel good about it. You think you *should* feel good about it, but you don't. So you think there must be something wrong with you!"

The bewilderment Nina expressed, which is common among movers, reflects the fact that the stresses of relocation are well kept secrets in our mobile society. Surges of distress following relocation can catch movers off guard and cause them to feel uncertain and ashamed.

Without question, there's a sunny side to moving. It can open up myriad new opportunities. But there's a shadow side too, and, in this chapter, we'll focus on that.

You may be tempted to skip over it, but we hope you won't. As a prospective mover, you need to understand the challenges you face—the emotional and social risks for you and your loved ones. You need to factor them into your decision about whether or not to move, and about when to move. Even if there's little choice, knowing what to expect can prevent you from being caught off guard and then doubting yourself. And it can help you develop strategies to deal with the challenges you'll face. In later chapters, we'll offer our own ideas about strategies to cope with the stresses we're describing now.

LOSSES

Whether people move reluctantly and fearfully or hopefully and joyfully, they usually expect to be making gains. Yet every entrance involves an exit. Every gain involves a loss. Whether felt before you move, immediately afterwards, or months later, grief and anxiety are almost inevitable in response to the myriad losses that a move entails. And, although it's certainly not inevitable, psychological depression is common too—a plunge in self-esteem cloaked in dark feelings of hopelessness, helplessness, worthlessness, futility, and fatigue. Here are the many reasons that can happen.

LOSING YOUR IDENTITY
Everyone has an inner sense of self. It's composed of mental images of your physical characteristics, capabilities, emotions, daydreams, values and goals. This sense of self defines for you, "This is who I am." It's always changing to some extent, but it has continuity too. There's a solid, familiar core of self that stays

constant over time. As this sense of self is outwardly expressed, it takes shape as identity—many identities, in fact, through which others know you and respond.

Most basically, identity is revealed through your physical being. When you encounter others—especially acquaintances and friends, they make comments such as, "You look wonderful!" "What a tan!" "You've lost weight," "That's a good-looking tie," "You're looking tired." The comments may not always be welcome, but they do affirm your identity. Others are noticing you, they know you exist, and they are probably glad you do.

The newcomer often feels unnoticed. "It was as though nobody saw me." "I was invisible." "I felt like a ghost," movers have said. This feeling of being invisible is eerie and deeply unsettling.

Your identity is also expressed and confirmed through the myriad social roles you play—roles that express your capabilities and give meaning to your life. Your central social identity—your work—may undergo little change in your move. Those of you who move to advance a career continue to be recognized as engineers, bankers, musicians. Traditionally, this has been especially true of male movers. Because of this continuity of identity, men are apt to be less deeply affected by a move then women. More women are moving for occupational reasons now, and their occupational identity is sustaining also.

To be sure, movers who are full-time homemakers also maintain their central roles as partner and parent. But their work is more fragmented and dispersed than business or a profession. It is usually more dependent on relationships in neighborhood and community.

Whether your central identity is in homemaking, business, or a profession, you are probably also involved in a web of connections—P.T.A., Little League, chamber of commerce, golf foursome, Friday night potluck suppers, theater group. For the committed, full-time professional, those roles may feel marginal. But for the homemaker, they are crucial. And that web of connection will be unraveled by a move.

Furthermore, your life has a familiar structure, shaped by the rhythms of work days, school days, partner's homecomings, and commitments to playmates, friends, and community.

"I feel very unsettled. I need things to be predictable. I need to have a routine. I feel very upset if I don't know what's coming next." This mover's distress has been expressed by many others. After a move, time and energy are needed to regain the familiar rhythms of daily life—the rhythms that are integral to your sense of self.

For the over-committed, the prospect of shedding some roles could feel like a relief. But there were reasons why you became over committed—perhaps you have unusually strong needs for involvement and recognition. Nearly everyone has those needs to some degree, and, for a span of time, they will be unfulfilled.

Moving is often caused by, or coincides with, a transition from one life phase, with its major identities, to another—the transition from student life to life in the workplace, from being single to being coupled, from being a child to being a parent, from being coupled to being widowed, from accustomed work to retirement. The stresses of role change and role loss are intensified.

"People here don't see me as an individual!" This was the voice of an offended newlywed whose move coincided with her transition into wifehood, and interrupted a budding career. "I'm outraged that people seem to see me only as the minister's wife who's expected to trail along behind. They ask how he's getting along but not how I'm getting along."

"I feel as though I'm floating—nobody here really knows who I am," said Jan, who had left her work in journalism to move with her husband and start a family. "It would have been different if I'd stayed in Houston. Sure, I might have given up the newspaper to be involved in full-time mothering for a while. But people would have still known me-the-editor."

"I always imagined that when I retired from the firm I'd move to a rural area where I could play a lot of golf," said Hank. "But I feel kind of empty now—nobody here knows me, and I feel sort of useless too."

Feeling invisible, unknown, or useless are lonely and frightening states. Losing certain of your identities—roles in which you've felt effective and have been appreciated by others—can be a serious threat to your self-esteem. It can pull you into a state of depression. That is an important psychological risk of moving.

LOSING SPECIAL PLACES

Your identities are also linked to the places that matter the most in your life. Your most special place is probably your home. Tiny apartment, trailer, or mansion, home is a shelter that feels safe, enfolding, strong, warm, and reliable. It's a place where you belong, a place where your taste, values, abilities, and emotions can be freely expressed and appreciated by others. Home is a place where relationships have developed and important experiences have occurred, so it's a place of memory, a place where your personal and family history are recorded.

If you feel deeply attached to your home, if your history and your feeling of continuity seem to be grounded in the physical structure, giving it up can nudge you into a state of psychological homelessness. You may feel sad, lost, and anxious for many months—or years.

Even if you've not been deeply attached to the physical dwelling, it is a realm in which you've probably felt competent. You know where things are, and how to make them work for dwelling yourself, your loved ones, and your friends. Moving ruptures that sense of mastery. It can be confusing, disorganizing, even chaotic. You may feel temporarily incompetent, and that may cause you to lose self-respect and slide into a depressive dip. People with strong needs for order, predictability, and control—there are many—are likely to feel most anxious and depressed during the transition.

Furthermore, if you relocate to a new community, it is likely that you will at first rent an apartment or house, and will go through the disruption of moving soon again.

If you carried out your Lifescan, you'll have identified other places that feel like extensions of your home—the woodland trail where you walk with your golden retriever, the coffee shop where you breakfast on your way to the office. When you leave those behind, you'll be leaving special parts of yourself. Although you will, hopefully, replace them, there will be moments of sadness and longing first.

LOSING SPECIAL PEOPLE

Your identities are closely connected to special people too.

"Every morning as I drove to work I would think, 'There isn't a single person in this town who really cares whether I'm here or not,'" Betsy remembered long after her move. Having nobody care is one of the deepest threats you can face.

Whereas for men, love partners are usually the most crucial source of caring—and love partners are likely to move with their men—most women need intimate friends as well.

"People here have been friendly from the start, but I have moments when I feel unbearably sad. I miss my dear friends so intensely," Jan said tearfully four months after her move. "With new people you're always having to prove yourself. Close friends accept you just as you are, good and bad." Leaving close friends is a major source of pain for women movers, whether single or coupled. It may take several years for new friendships to deepen, and during that interlude there may be rebuffs and disappointments that will cause you to wonder if you're really a likable person. More bruises to your self-esteem.

And what about others in whom you confide—your clergy person, your doctor, your hairdresser? People who "accept you just as you are, good and bad," in Jan's words. People who understand you, encourage you, comfort you. You'll miss them grievously for a while.

Your parents, brothers and sisters, grown-up children—what about leaving them? That may be more complicated than leaving friends. You may feel relieved to get away if your kin have been too nosy or bossy. But you may feel guilty if you believe they need you. Or you may feel worried if you believe you need them. Almost surely there will be threads of sorrow mingled among the other feelings.

Another of our Myths of Moving is that important relationships can be fully preserved by letter and phone. For sure, they can be sustained. But we communicate with movement, with touch, with smiles, frowns, and glances, even with smells. It's rare that letters and phone calls can take the place of all that.

Moving is permeated with loss, and you may find yourself awash with troubled feelings. You may feel angry. You may feel fearful. You may feel disappointed in yourself. You'll almost certainly feel grief—sadness and longing for what you've lost.

It's quite appropriate for you to grieve over your losses. Some movers grieve so intensely that they compare the experience to bereavement.

Unfortunately, your new community may be reluctant to know about the sadness you're feeling.

"We have to wear our having-a-good-time masks when we go to gatherings." "Everybody seems to be all smiles and happiness at being here. They insist that you like it here." "The mood I'm in, people wouldn't want me around. I'm a real downer." These are movers' voices.

Why should your new community recoil from your grief? For several reasons. Settled residents, unless they were born there, have struggled through their own transitional pain. They have made connections in the community, and reached a state of equilibrium. The newcomer's distress can disturb that equilibrium, threatening to reawaken forgotten (and unwelcome) sadness. Or—enmeshed in the needs and commitments of their own lives—they may have failed to reach out to the newcomer. His or her sadness and loneliness can arouse their guilt and cause them to turn away. Or they may feel helpless to assuage the grief, and recoil from that uncomfortable feeling too.

But it won't be easy for you to wear a "having-a-good time" mask when your mood is blue and your energy is at a low ebb.

RISKS TO YOUR LOVE PARTNERSHIP

Your relationship with your partner will be challenged by your move. Especially if you're in the corporate world, it's likely that you'll be separated from each other at moving time— perhaps for many weeks. You won't share the crisis of transition.

Then, as individuals and as a couple, you'll be separated from familiar, trustworthy sources of comfort and validation— friends, relatives, colleagues, clergy people, health professionals. So, once you've both moved, you'll want to turn to each other for fulfillment of needs intensified by the move—the need to be understood, the need to be soothed, the need for recognition. And you'll have only each other to hear about the powerful emotions the move may stir up. There's likely to be a turning in on yourselves that could deepen your relationship, but could also overburden it.

Traditionally, a couple was likely to move to further a man's occupation. This has changed. Now, the accompanying partner may be a man, supporting a woman's career advancement. Or both partners—whether they have formed an opposite-sex couple or a same-sex couple—may move to accept new opportunities, or to seek a new lifestyle. It's still likely, though, that there will be a skew in their satisfaction, so let's consider how that may be played out.

If you are the accompanying partner, the move may stir up resentment, envy, and anger towards your partner. First, the losses involved in a move can be painful, and you will probably feel twinges of resentment towards the cause of your pain—the partner who most wanted to move.

Next, you may be enduring a hurtful feeling of invisibility in your new community while your partner is being warmly recognized as the new teacher, the new vice-president. While you're on your own, your partner may be surrounded by staff or colleagues to welcome, support, and orient him or her. While you're feeling that you're accomplishing nothing, s/he may come home glowing with excitement and fulfillment. You're swamped by loss while your partner is basking in gain.

You may feel abandoned because the balance of your relationship has been disturbed. As one or both becomes immersed in a new workplace, or develops new roles in the community, each may have less than usual time, energy, or interest available for the other.

Traditionally, when married couples have moved the woman has been charged with the social and psychological work of transition. In one husband's words, "It's my job to get my promotion; it's your job to adjust." "Adjusting" meant supporting the children and him through their times of worry and doubt, and being content while she did it. He only hinted at his own fear that he might not be successful, yet every mover faces that risk in a new workplace. It causes intense preoccupation with the new work, and maybe some sleepless nights.

Unfortunately, new jobs don't always work out. The project may be different from what was described, the boss' expectations may be unreasonable, colleagues may be fiercely competitive. Three months after his move, John's firm ran into financial problems and threatened to break his contract. "John was beside himself," his wife remembered. "He said 'Maybe we should never have come here.' I didn't want to hear that. I just went horizontal."

If the partner who wanted the job change isn't successful, not only is s/he faced with loss of self-respect but also with guilt for having let the family down. The other partner must struggle with reproachful feelings and unspoken thoughts—"After all we went through, you couldn't make a go of it."

For all those reasons, you may have dark feelings towards your partner. But, because you love him or her, those feelings are unwelcome. They may not fit your image of who you are. So they leave you feeling guilty towards your mate and ashamed of yourself—another drag toward depression.

You may try to hide your feelings from your partner. Many women see their men as emotionally fragile and assume a protective role. Many men have been reared to be stoical and not let on when they're hurting. But it's likely that your troubled feelings will leak out in the expression on your face, the way you hold your body, the tone of your voice. Your partner may then feel guilty for having burdened you with the move, or resentful because your pain makes him/her so uncomfortable.

It's possible, of course, that you don't really know what you feel, especially if those emotions don't conform to your ideals for yourself. You may simply feel cranky or in the dumps. One reason we write this is to help you put a name to your unwelcome and painful feelings. Unless these emotions can be understood and constructively expressed, they can start a spiral of estrangement.

RISKS TO YOUR CHILDREN

A move can be stressful for children at any age. But if you recognize the factors that can make them vulnerable to adverse effects, you'll be able to develop strategies to help them grow through their move. Here we'll identify the risks. Later we'll focus on the strategies.

Although most children are adaptable and resilient, exposure to multiple strains can overwhelm them. So, as you consider moving, it's wise to identify other stresses your child may be dealing with already—the birth of a sibling, a serious illness or death in the family, separation or divorce of parents, for example. Recognizing those stresses may influence the timing of your move—or whether you move at all.

If you are separated or divorced, it's important to consider how a move will shape your child's relationship with his/her other parent. If you are a single parent, think about the people who are specially supportive to your child and to you in your parenting role—grandparents, aunts, uncles, close friends.

Take into account any special needs your child may have. For example, there may be a need for special medical or educational resources that couldn't easily be found in another community.

And keep in mind that whatever affects you will affect your children. If your move stirs sadness, anxiety, or depression in you or your partner, you may find it difficult to be responsive to your children at a time when their needs are heightened. It may be hard to listen sympathetically to their thoughts and feelings, to reassure and encourage them, and to help them figure out solutions to their problems.

These things are important for children of all ages. But the impact of a move will vary with their ages and developmental stages.

INFANTS AND PRE-SCHOOL CHILDREN

A very young child's world is small. It's usually possible to transport the cocoon that helps him or her feel secure—your presence, familiar furniture and playthings, trusted pets. But it's not always simple. Within weeks after birth, babies begin noticing colors, shapes, similarities and differences. And, increasingly, they notice changes.

"When I was packing, Sue was actually looking for her things," said Judy, recalling her move with her nine month old daughter. "She was beginning to kind of talk and she was pointing, so I knew she was looking for her teddy bear or her shelf of books. She got very irritable. I'd pack a box and she'd unpack it like she didn't want me to pack. Sue's a very sensitive, deliberate kind of kid, and she was taking the stuff back out and crawling over and putting it back where she thought it should go. Without talking, she was telling me an awful lot."

"After we got there and unloaded the truck, I set up her room. I set up her bookshelf the way it had been set up at home, and her crib, and the line of stuffed animals. Until I did that I think she was really anxious."

This swift re-creation of her familiar cocoon reassured nine month old Sue. When Ralph moved at two and a half, his mother, Ellen, tried to do the same.

"While he was in daycare, I spent the day preparing his room," she recalled. "He came home to his new room with all his familiar things in it. But it backfired! He was completely confused. He needed to see how it happened. He needed to see the truck, to see who carried the boxes."

Although the child between two and five has more resources to deal with change than an infant, there are vulnerabilities then too. In this age-span, children find it hard to separate fantasy from reality. They are likely to embellish what they learn about an impending move, and imagine a frightening scenario. For Ralph, having his room reappear in a new, strange place must have seemed like magic and—being beyond our understanding and control—magic can be scary. Fortunately for Ralph, Ellen understood his confusion. And she had the time and resources to help him work through a step-by-step transition.

"He needed to say good-bye. He needed a dozen trips back to our old house. At first we went into the house, then he peeked through the window, then it was enough to drive by. He missed the trees. He even missed the bugs!"

Both Ralph and Sue—different ages, different sexes, different families—showed intense attachment to place. Sue, like most children, reacted to her awareness of outer change with behavioral changes—clinging, crying, more wakefulness at night. Older children may become more babyish—using baby talk, wetting the bed, soiling their underpants again—or become irritable and negativistic.

What's the risk? Won't this pass? Yes, if a parent can respond constructively to the signals of distress (we'll suggest strategies later), it's probable that the child will recover in a few weeks or months (it took Sue one month). But if you've run out of steam yourself because of the move, a downward spiral can be set into motion. If your child's behavior makes you cranky and impatient, s/he will sense your worrisome moods and respond with even more clinging, whining, and tears, which will cause you more frustration and discouragement—and on it goes. That's when long-term problems develop.

Young children are also especially vulnerable to accidents after a move. That may be because the surroundings are strange—no longer does s/he know where things are and how they work. Or it may be that the caregiver is preoccupied or overwhelmed. It takes only a moment alone in the bathtub to threaten an infant's life. It takes only a moment alone in the kitchen for a toddler to pull a steaming saucepan off the stove.

So helping even a baby or toddler through a move is a challenge for parents. But only a minority of American families now include two married parents with children under eighteen. And fewer than one in ten include a full-time, stay-at-home mom like Ellen and Judy (we don't yet know how many such fathers there are—it's a growing number). Many pre-schoolers are being looked after in day care centers or by nannies.

It's easy to minimize a small child's attachment to caregivers outside the family. Yet many babies clearly distinguish between their caregivers by the middle of their first year of life. Many clearly signal which caregiver they prefer. And it's through the reliable, appropriate, and affectionate responses of the primary caregivers (parental and paid) that a young child develops the trust that is the foundation of personal security and self-esteem.

The rupture of close attachments to their caregivers can have a strong impact on your children. So while you are grieving your losses after your move, your baby or toddler will be grieving her/his own.

ELEMENTARY SCHOOL-AGE CHILDREN:

During the elementary school years, many children can take a move in stride. But their sense of loss and disconnection can still be intense.

"We moved here in August, when Ralph was five and a half," Ellen recalls. "It was his fourth move by then. One night we went to a restaurant to get some pie. We didn't know exactly when school started, and we weren't sure who to ask. When the waiter came, he looked as though he might know. But he didn't, and he said, 'Don't you know anyone you can ask?' Ralph looked up, and he said, 'No, we don't. We're the lonely family.'"

"My most difficult move was between grades three and four," Janice recalls. "I cried every night all summer. I never told my parents what was wrong, and they didn't connect it with moving."

"I was very attached to our neighborhood. The kids would come into our back yard and call—a certain call was a coded invitation to come out and play. There was a lot of informal play on the street—marbles, ball, things like that."

"A different neighborhood meant a different school, different kinds of kids. They went to dancing school, all dressed up and with white gloves. I didn't like that. I didn't fit in. I didn't make friends for at least a year."

Janice felt alienated from the culture of her new school—the different behavior, values and expectations.

"There *is* a real culture in childhood," Ellen confirms. ''When we lived on a military base in the south the kids were all involved with Mutant Ninja Turtles. My son wore turtle t-shirts and slept in turtle p.j.s. I quickly realized that this Vermont community wouldn't tolerate the violence in that. He'd be seen as an outsider, and, as his mother, I would too."

Although the emotional bonds of elementary school children are still grounded in their families, they may also feel attached to special places and special people, and to the symbols of those attachments—from coded calls to Mutant Ninja Turtles. Rupturing those bonds can stir sadness, loneliness, confusion, and anxiety, both before and after a move. Being alert to that possibility can help you respond to your child's troubled moods or behavior with understanding and support.

And be alert to the academic challenge of changing schools. It's during the elementary years that the building blocks of formal learning are laid down—especially the "Three R's." If the tasks in the new school are more advanced, and your children lose a connecting link, they are apt to flounder. If the work is less advanced, they may be bored. Here's another realm in which you may need to be your child's advocate.

ADOLESCENTS

During the junior high and high school years, youngsters can be very vulnerable to adverse effects from their moves. Some of the challenges they face are important for younger children too, but the significance of those issues intensifies during the teens. And adolescence presents special issues of its own.

Loss of Mastery A central responsibility of parents is to help your children become competent adults who will be able to negotiate their own course through life. Hopefully, your children will grow increasingly effective in influencing and responding to the people and things in their world. As they experience a growing sense of mastery, their self-esteem becomes more secure.

When a family moves, it's usually the parents who make the decision. A child's vote is often uncounted (we'll come back to this in Chapter 5). So your youngsters may experience moving as a major loss of control over their lives. And the move plunges them into new realms of the world that must be mastered. Just as you may feel helpless, anxious, and confused, they may too.

For the teenager, the challenge is compounded. Adolescence is a time of rapid growth and sexual maturation yet the youngsters' mastery of their aggressive and sexual urges is insecure. It's a stormy passage most successfully traveled when there is consistency, reliability, and familiarity in the outer world.

Unfortunately, a major move strips away consistency, reliability, and familiarity. Relocated teenagers must deal with massive external change on top of inner turbulence. Their sense of mastery is challenged intensely, and this happens just as they are struggling to feel competent on their own, independently of their parents.

Lost identity is a crucial issue for teen movers too. Adolescence is a time of self-questioning and doubt, and fluctuating self-esteem. "Who am I, who do I want to become, and am I a worthwhile person?" are central questions.

Although identity is at first anchored in the family, outside sources of recognition matter more and more. Teens are recognized, and their specialness is validated, by other youngsters and myriad adults outside the family: teachers, coaches, Scout leaders, crossing guards, school bus drivers, librarians and shopkeepers in the neighborhood store. "New kids on the block" aren't recognized at first—they may experience the same devastating feeling of invisibility that you risk when you move. Or they may be recognized, but only as one who doesn't belong.

"You have to invent a new me every time you move," said fifteen-year-old Chris. "It's because the kids are so different." That can feel like an opportunity or a threat. For some youngsters, the changes increase confusion about who they really are. For Janice, who moved in the middle of junior high, it was an opportunity.

"That summer, my cousin took me under her wing. She taught me how to do my hair and gave me an introduction into being a teen. And when I started in the new school, I felt I could leave some of my foibles behind." Being "born" into a new identity as teen was a positive move for her.

Much of adolescence, of course, is about "inventing a new me"—trying out new roles and relationships as the maturing self takes shape. But the "new me" needs models to emulate. S/he needs reactions that help her/him develop a realistic view of capabilities and limitations. And the "new me" needs a sense of belonging. S/he needs acceptance outside of the family. So another threat for the young mover is losing friends.

Loss of Friends Friends can mean many things—from the gang that hangs out in the mall on Saturday night to the confidante who knows every secret fear and wish. They play many roles (described in Chapter 2), helping people feel understood, cared about, and supported.

Friends help people feel they belong. For the teenager, this is crucial. Teens in our country are expected to differentiate from their families, temporarily rejecting family behavior, beliefs, and values. But as teens feel more distinct, more independent from the family (the need for separateness is less intense in girls), a sense of sameness with age mates is urgently needed. Feeling different from them can be lonely and frightening. Yet a newcomer *is* different just because s/he is new.

To be sure, every student entering junior high or high school is a newcomer, but alliances from elementary school and neighborhood friends can ease the transition. Cliques form quickly, and youngsters may close ranks against the incoming mover. There may be the bewildering hurt of quiet exclusion, or the wounds of open insults and physical aggression. In either case, the newcomer feels lonely and wonders forlornly, "What's wrong with me?" And if the culture—the ethnic or socioeconomic mix, the dominant modes of behavior, speech, and dress—in the new school differs from the newcomer's previous school, the feeling of being an outsider is intensified.

To win the acceptance that they long for, youngsters may need, or believe they need, some special quality or talent. For Steve, uprooted repeatedly by his high-tech father's career, it was skill in soccer that quickly earned him kudos. For Janice, it was talent on the violin that smoothed her junior high school move.

But keeping up high levels of achievement can be a strain. And what of the youngster without a special talent? In many high schools, the most accomplished students form closely-knit groups. The "looser" coalitions—the ones in which students drift in and out—are apt to include youngsters who feel marginal and behave in marginal ways. These are the coalitions in which drinking and drug use may be rampant. They are the ones that may be most receptive to the newcomer.

Love Relationships Although friendships provide a safe harbor for sharing the mysteries, questions, fears, and excitement of sexual development, adolescence is also the time of trial love relationships. Often sexual, which are forerunners of later commitment to a mate.

There are strong pressures on youngsters to become sexually active before they feel emotionally ready. In such cases, interruption of a relationship can be welcome. But the rupture of a love partnership through moving can also cause deep pain. It can lead to an unrealistic idealization of a relationship that would otherwise have been outgrown. Or it may spur the adolescent to make a premature commitment after the move, clutching onto a new love partner as though s/he were a life raft in a stormy sea.

Parental Survival There's one more thing to consider about moving with your teenager. For you to survive—let alone enjoy—your youngster's adolescence, you need to feel resilient and steadfast. Unfortunately, his/her phase of turbulence—with its challenges of your authority and values, with the waves of hostility or scorn that your teenager may pour over you—is likely to coincide with a life phase when you are experiencing self-doubt: fears of losing physical vigor or sexual attractiveness, questions about your accomplishments, uncertainty about the meaning of your life. Adding on a major move may be an overload.

In this chapter we've explored the shadow side of moving—social and emotional risks that are hard for you to read about. Yet facing them squarely can help you make a wise decision. It can help you develop effective strategies if you do decide to move.

The next step, though, is to learn about the community that may become your new home.

Chapter 3 Exercises

EXERCISE A

Think of someone you know well—a friend, relative, or a colleague—who has recently moved. In what ways would you describe the impact of moving on that person?

What were the positive ("sunny side") outcomes?

_____

_____

What were the negative ("shadow side") outcomes?

_____

_____

EXERCISE B

If you have moved before, either as an adult or as a child, think about the impact of moving on yourself:

What was the "sunny side"?

_____

_____

What was the "shadow side"?

_____

_____

EXERCISE C

Look at the list of nouns you chose to describe yourself in the Chapter 2 exercise, particularly the five most important. How will the move affect you in each of those five different roles?

EXERCISE D

How will the move affect your ability to visit your six favorite places?

_____

_____

EXERCISE E

Think about times in your adult life when you were a new student, employee, neighbor, partner, or parent. Can you recall:

How did it feel to be new?

_____

_____

Who greeted you, helped you with questions or problems, took care of you?

_____

_____

In what ways did you take care of yourself during the transition?

_____

_____

EXERCISE F

Think about the most recent major transition in your life—perhaps you've begun or ended a love relationship, retired, become a full-time parent, taken a new job. In the "crisis of transition":

How did you feel (or still feel) about the changes in your life?"

_____

_____

What were the sunny sides and shadow sides?

_____

_____

Who helped and took care of you through the transition? In what ways were you taken care of?

_____

_____

In what ways did you take care of yourself in the transition?

_____

_____

CHAPTER 4

Explore the "Maybe" Places

"I haven't a clue how you go about finding out about a new community," Pru, the savvy young wife of a physician in training, said as she contemplated a move. Perplexity like hers, not uncommon among movers, arises because we rarely pause to clarify our needs. We can't find answers until we understand the questions.

Hopefully, exploring your motives for moving, and scanning the realms of your life, have helped you identify your own questions. Now it is time to find out if a new environment is likely to foster your security, effectiveness, significance, and your capacity for work and love.

"Why bother?" you may ask. "We have to move." Pru's husband had to move on to finish his training. But there were medical centers in three different regions to which he could apply. The life of the family would be shaped by the community they chose.

"I have no choice," you may insist. "If I don't accept this promotion and move to Ohio, I'll be edged out of the company." You have no choice? Are you certain that your present career track is the one you really want? Perhaps it is. Or maybe the job market's too shaky to consider a change. So Ohio it is. But you do have choices—where to live, where to play, where to worship, where to educate your children if you have them.

"Why not find out after I get there?" you ask. You could—if risks turn you on, if you savor the unknown, if you bounce back easily from disappointments. And if you're moving alone, so only your own contentment is at stake.

But most people face the known more confidently than the unknown. For most people, knowing is a way of feeling competent, and feeling competent is a foundation of self-esteem. And for most people, information contributes to making wise choices.

GATHERING INFORMATION IN ADVANCE

How might you learn about an unfamiliar community? Why not start with your local librarian? S/he is likely to be an expert in the realm of information retrieval, familiar with new computer technology. You might supplement the library's sources of information with materials requested from the chamber of commerce of the new community, its town hall, the League of Women Voters, and a major realtor. And why not send for the local newspapers? From these sources, you could gather information about climate, population characteristics, cost of living and real estate values, recreational and cultural facilities, the political climate, level of street crime and a great deal more.

From the yellow pages in the new community's phone books, which the librarian might help you procure, you could gather addresses of organizations that are important in your life: women's organizations (informational, legal and counseling services); health care providers; child care resources; school administrations; churches. They probably have newsletters or pamphlets that can be yours for the asking.

In the travel section of your library or bookstore you'll find guide books full of information about the region or city you are considering.

Your school or college alumni/ae association, your business or professional association, and your church or synagogue may provide the names of members living in that area—people you could write or call, and who would be willing to talk frankly about its pros and cons.

Finally, if you have E-mail and access to Internet, there's a wealth of information waiting to be gathered. But frame your questions carefully or you may learn more than you ever wanted to know!

♤

VISITING THE PROSPECTIVE COMMUNITY

At least one exploratory visit to the new place is important—more than one if you have the time and money. The value of your visit will be proportionate to your clarity of purpose and the precision of your questions: "What am I trying to find out?" you need to ask yourself in advance. "What is most important in my life?" Here again, your Lifescan can be helpful, in conjunction with the information you've been gathering. Why not summarize the most important points, making up an outline or checklist to take with you?

On your visit, you may want a guide—a prospective colleague, a friend of a friend, maybe a realtor—or you may prefer to rent a car, get some local maps, and drive around on your own. (Before you set out alone, it could be wise to contact the police, and find out if there are any sections that are unsafe on foot or even in a car.) Then try to get an overview, exploring different sections of the community at different times of day. Are there trees, public gardens, parks? Do you see open space and light, or narrow canyons between tall buildings? Do you hear a cacophony of noises, or a tranquil hum? What do you smell—newly mown grass, pizza, diesel exhaust?

Notice the flow of traffic between various residential areas, your prospective workplace, and the schools, as well as the quality of public transportation. Notice provisions for cyclists, joggers and walkers. Are there sidewalks? Bike lanes? Are they in use?

What are you feeling as you drive around—exhilaration, dread, indifference? Make some notes. You may not remember.

SCANNING HOMES

The place you live in may be the center of your new life. So study the types of housing and their relationship to the land—are units clustered together or secluded? Notice the age range and ethnic characteristics of the people in various neighborhoods, as well as their styles of outdoor interaction. Is there a porch life, a yard life, a street life, or are people shielded from view? Which style do you prefer?

When you locate appealing neighborhoods, you might saunter around and chat with householders about local customs and lifestyles. For every householder who may find your knock on the door intrusive, another may find it welcome, and enjoy the chance to be a local "authority."

Hopefully, your Lifescan has helped you identify the characteristics you want in a new apartment or house: more rooms or fewer than you now have, a certain kind of room arrangement, a particular orientation to the sun, a special sort of view, closeness to or distance from the neighbors, space for a garden, a welcome for pets.

So now, with a realtor, you can investigate homes for rent or sale, using your checklist, a tape measure, sketch pad, and camera to bolster your memory. Keep in mind that what you see during your visit may change when the seasons change. If sunlight is important to buoy your mood, notice whether the trees are deciduous or evergreen, and how they will affect the light when winter (or summer) comes. If visual privacy is important, will that change after the leaves have fallen? (We're stressing the psychological and social aspects of your move. Your library or realtor can supply you with detailed guides to house hunting.)

"We'll rent something for a while, and then find what we really want," you may think. Be cautious here. True, an occasional person dismantles a home and re-creates it with unflagging confidence and cheer. For most, as we've described in Chapter 3, there is confusion and temporary helplessness. And since your self-esteem is grounded in feeling competent and effective, that chaotic interlude can threaten the self-esteem of everyone in the family. It can breed anxiety and depression. Even changing neighborhoods within the same town can rupture neighborly connections and budding friendships, and may involve a new school district for your children. So it's good strategy to minimize repeated disruptions, especially by avoiding short-term rentals.

Few people can live in Camelot. Lives are filled with compromise. But gathering information carefully during an advance visit can protect you from having your daydreams shattered after you've moved, when you are especially vulnerable.

Polly's daydream was shattered. During her visit to a New England town where there was a school of engineering that her husband was considering, she was entranced.

"It seemed magical. The foliage was brilliant in October. It was close to Maine and lobster, we had heard about the Connecticut river and the prospect of canoeing, we ski and we like the mountains, the training program seemed excellent, the air was cold, and I imagined being in front of a fire. And the colonial architecture was appealing."

She longed for one of those colonial houses, dreaming of how she would decorate it to express her taste and her interest in folk art.

"We had a copy of the newspaper sent to us," she said, "and we studied the real estate ads. There were attractive houses that seemed affordable. We didn't realize they were miles out in the boonies." This capable woman hadn't thought to procure a map or write a letter of inquiry to realtors advertising their properties. Even during her visit, Polly hadn't discovered that the attractive houses close to her husband's workplace were not affordable.

For the next three years, Polly lived in a prefabricated house she termed "the shack." Adding insult to injury, it was cold. She hadn't thought to ask about the cost of fuel for heating. Too late, she found the price was so high that she and her student husband needed to keep the thermostat set below their comfort level during the long winter.

FINDING OUT ABOUT FOOD

Closely linked to home, food nourishes in many ways. Every person and every family prefers foods that symbolize emotional security and comfort—special breads or soups or cozy mashed potatoes. Everyone feels connected to foods that evoke memories of family rituals and traditions. And many people express and confirm their ethnic roots by serving and enjoying foods with special religious or cultural meaning

Jacob, a thirty-seven-year-old newcomer, felt unexpectedly shaken when he went into a Vermont country store for provisions for his family's traditional Sunday breakfast. "Do you have lox?" he asked the shopkeeper, after searching among the overflowing shelves. "Why, I sure do," the Vermonter answered. "Go to the end of this aisle, pass the next, and they're halfway down the one after." Jacob did that. But the array of hardware that faced him, including four kinds of locks, was not what he hoped to put on his bagels that day.

If certain foods have special meanings for you, it's easy to inquire about a French bakery, a Jewish delicatessen—whatever you prize—during your visit. Find out about particular restaurants too. The tantalizing aroma of favorite foods—maybe sun-drenched tomato, garlic, and oregano on pizza—can help you feel reconnected after your move.

EXPLORING WORK

A new job or promotion is likely to be a central reason for moving. Hopefully, you will have gathered information about the workplace you're considering. You will have talked with faculty and advisors in your school or college, contacted alumni/ae who may know the organization, talked with your present colleagues, learned more about the reputation of the firm from professional and business publications.

Look back at Chapter 1 and remind yourself what you're anxious to change in your work situation. Being clear about that will help you ask focused questions in your interviews. Even if this is the only job available now, you may decide to try it out before relocating your family.

People sometimes suppose that moving will provide a natural opportunity to change their field of work. It can do that. It can open up new vistas, engaging talents you've never used before. But the confluence of so much change can be overwhelming, too. If possible, it can be wiser to make the transitions at separate times, either postponing a move until the work change feels comfortable, or carrying the continuity of familiar work into the new locale.

If you're moving to further your partner's career, what about work for you? More than men, coupled women are lax about exploring that realm. Yet women need recognition outside their households too. Whether it's part-time or full-time, paid or voluntary—whether the work is selling homemade Greek pastries, raising funds for a shelter for the homeless, or doing biochemical research—it offsets the feeling of invisibility that movers find so troubling.

So try now to identify a sphere of satisfying and visible work that you can continue after your move, and find out whether or not there will be opportunities in the new community to do that work. Even before you visit, you may uncover possibilities through your professional or business associations, through magazine and newspapers ads, through newsletters of voluntary organizations, through the human resource office of your partner's prospective firm. And then make inquiries at every opportunity during your visit.

If your primary work is homemaking, you may underplay the complexity of your role, imagining "I can do this anywhere." That's another of the Myths of Moving. Don't believe it. Rather, ask yourself what and who supports you in being effective in the domestic sphere, and who supplies you with needed recognition? That's responsible self-care. During your visit, try to learn where you could find new colleagues-in-parenting. Are there parent groups, mothering centers, children's programs at the library or community center where parents gather too?

SCOUTING SCHOOLS

Are you committed to public education, or open to parochial or private schools if the public schools don't meet your standards? Can you afford to consider those choices? Do they have waiting lists? Or are you thinking of home schooling? Try to sort out those questions before you visit. Then find out what school district your child would be in. Ask the superintendent's office for materials prepared for parents, and the P.T.O. newsletter. Ask to visit the school your child may attend, and set up a conference with a member of the administration.

What might you want to find out in your conference? We'll share a few ideas—you'll have many of your own. Perhaps start with funding. Is there state funding, or do the schools depend on local property taxes? Is the budget stable, or continually under attack? Is there support for foreign language classes and extra-curricular activities such as sports, music, field trips? Is there support for continuing education for teachers?

How many students are in a class? Are students with different levels of ability separated into streams, or all taught together? What programs are available for children with special needs?

What proportion of students are newcomers each year? How are they welcomed into the school?

What proportion of students are college bound? Technical school bound? What proportion drop out?

Are there problems with drugs, alcohol, violence, pregnancy? How are they dealt with by the school?

What's the role of the P.T.O—tutoring, fund-raising, chaperoning, helping develop special aspects of the curriculum such as sex and family life education?

Will the school cooperate if you plan on home schooling? Is there a local branch of the Home School Educators Association? A good library?

SEARCHING FOR OTHER SPECIAL PLACES

Where will you and your children play? You may not need to see each baseball field and swimming pool, science museum and concert hall. You will want to know if they're there. Are they accessible by foot and bike as well as bus and car? Are they in a zone of safety or of danger? Are they open to the community, or restricted to members? Can you afford the fees?

You'll need those play spaces to renew yourselves, but they're just as important in another way too. They are the places where people gather, and meeting people will have a high priority.

It's strange to think of making friends as a purposeful act. But once school days are past, with their inevitable interactions in work and play, opportunities to be among people who share your interests have to be created. So find out about the gathering places where informal, repeated encounters can occur, where you'll begin to recognize others and be recognized. Do people gather on neighborhood sidewalks or convenience stores, at the salad bar in the supermarket, in coffee houses, parks, or playgrounds? Where do kids head in their leisure hours? Are there neighborhood pickup basketball games? Are they hanging out in the mall? Are those places safe?

Why not go to the riverside park, the ice-cream shop, and see how it feels? As a stranger, are you noticed? Do people meet your gaze and smile? Do they speak to you or your child (your dog's a fine ice-breaker, but she probably had to stay home)? Or do they avoid eye contact and turn away? You'll learn a lot about how newcomers are welcomed there.

And what about the church or synagogue? Why not meet with the pastor or rabbi and learn how newcomers are gathered in?

You'll come away from your visit(s) with myriad impressions and some notes, photos, and phone numbers for follow-up calls (see our appendix also). Then you'll need to sort it out. You'll need to look at the information you've gathered in relation to your reasons for moving, your Lifescan, and the risks that we've brought into focus. In what ways, you should ask yourself, would moving to this place change my life, diminish my life, enrich my life?

RESEARCH FOR RETIREMENT

The population of seniors is increasing, and many moves are prompted by retirement. Movers approaching retirement age may feel clear about the elements in their lives that give it special zest. But they may not take into account the changes that retirement will cause, nor the stress of simultaneous retirement and moving.

Yet there are special aspects of a new community that the mover who has retired, or is approaching retirement, should consider. These are based on issues associated with aging. Considering them can help you decide whether you will feel more secure in a retirement community in which all the inhabitants share the needs and concerns of aging, or whether you will feel more vitalized and comforted in a mixed community where you can interact with younger people outside of your family. If your offspring are relocating, your research can help you decide whether or not to move to the same community.

FACING LOSSES

First, in addition to losses faced by movers of any age—loss of identity, loss of special people and special places—the older mover is likely to face the loss of some physical capabilities. (If possible, this should be counterbalanced by continuing growth in other spheres—new knowledge, new forms of self-expression, new contributions to society.)

Second, the older mover faces the bleak prospect of the death of a partner and/or other loved ones. (As much as possible, this needs to be offset by continuing connection to younger family members and friends.)

Third, the older mover—except for a privileged minority—faces a reduction of financial resources. (This must be offset by a shift towards activities and facilities that are available at little or no cost.)

If these are among the major issues, what characteristics of a prospective community need to be researched by the older mover, beyond those which are important for all movers?

Loss of physical capabilities can often be minimized or postponed if the older mover stays physically active. What facilities and programs for swimming, bicycling, cross-country skiing, racquet sports, low-demand dance and rhythmic movement and yoga are available in the prospective community, and at what expense? Is it safe to walk? In the north, sidewalks are icy in winter. Is the older walker at risk for a fractured hip? Is the older walker at risk for being assaulted? Or is there a secure indoor track, perhaps in a shopping mall?

Are there professionals committed to preserving health—fitness trainers, physical therapists, massage therapists, nutritionists, nurse practitioners, as well as physicians? Sound guidance about nutrition and exercise can help stave off heart disease and control arthritis among both men and women. For women, it can prevent or reduce the scourge of osteoporosis (the thinning and increased brittleness of bones that often follows menopause and results in many a fracture). Mammography and the pap smear for women, rectal exams for men and women are essential to detect early cancers. Are such procedures available and affordable?

In spite of health-sustaining efforts, some loss of physical capabilities is likely to occur. Is safe, affordable housing available with ready access (a level driveway and entry, one-story living quarters)?

It has been convincingly shown that pets offer both physical and psychological benefits for the elderly. Will the housing code allow pets to be in residence?

When it becomes risky to drive a car, will an efficient, safe system of public transportation be available? Will there be easy physical access to shopping, recreational facilities, the library, the new workplace?

Illness will inevitably occur. What medical care is available for the older person who is probably on a reduced income? Are there physicians with a particular interest in the care of aging patients?

What hospitals, nursing homes, day-care programs, outreach programs will be available if physical or mental capabilities fail seriously? What possibilities are there for preserving the connection between an ailing spouse and a healthy spouse? And are there hospice programs for the time of dying?

Since the prospect of death often gives new urgency to a religious affiliation, is there a church whose teachings are compatible with your own beliefs? Will it be physically accessible?

Death of loved ones, whether spouse or dear friends, is inevitable. This fact should cause a prospective mover to pause and consider deeply the wisdom of uprooting. Is the time when you face the possible loss of your nearest and dearest a wise time to sever connections with a supportive network of long-time friends and colleagues? Or do you need to move to build a network of supportive people?

Your may wish to re-establish past connections by moving closer to your offspring or other family members. Especially if you've been widowed, that can be an appealing prospect. It's a risky one too. What if that son or daughter decides to move away? Is she or he deeply enough rooted so that is unlikely? Would you be prepared to make another move?

MAKING GAINS

There's much more to aging than loss, illness and death. There is the possibility of counterbalancing loss with gain. You can sustain your intellectual, political and cultural interests and, hopefully, develop new ones both with your partner and on your own.

Moving towards these goals, you might investigate the availability of libraries and university courses. Explore the possibility of participating in workshops and performing groups as a writer, singer, actor, painter, potter, weaver. Inquire about groups dedicated to political, social, and environmental interests, such as conservation or nuclear disarmament. There is as much place in the Sierra Club, for example, for someone willing to make calls about legislation as someone interested in technical rock climbing. Within such organizations, you can develop new connections with people of all ages. You can develop a new "family" of people with shared concerns.

Try to explore new opportunities for work, paid or unpaid, to maintain your sense of significance. Some communities have organizations through which retired business and professional workers provide consultation to inexperienced ones. Some match the talents of older volunteers with unmet human needs. Here is a realm in which you can surely sustain your connection with the young. Like Phil, a retired Marine officer, you might discover the nurturing side of your personality by holding and soothing sick babies in the hospital. You might become a proxy grandparent to "latchkey" children who go home to an empty house, phoning and asking warmly, "How was your day?" You might tutor a child having problems with math, or be a reliable presence in a daycare center. Some calls to the church, the school superintendent, and the hospital volunteer office will give you an idea of what's being done—and what needs to be developed.

The psychological work of moving tends to be done primarily by women. And the dispersion of women's roles in their earlier years may lead to more possibilities at retirement age than men envision. So, if you're coupled with a man, encourage your partner—whose life will no longer be organized around his primary occupation—to seek the same sorts of information for himself. You may need to help him search for new occupations and meanings in his life, some shared with you, some separate. Exploring a prospective community together can stimulate you both to start doing that.

Chapter 4 Exercises

EXERCISE A

There are always some opportunities to make significant choices about *if, where, when,* and *how* you'll move. The information you gather as you research a new community can be used to identify choices and make important decisions.

We encourage you to discuss your responses to items in the following exercise with your partner, and/or a friend. You might find it useful, too, to look over these questions with a recent mover. Sometimes others' hindsights can become our own valuable foresights!

As I recall past moves, I felt as though I had few or no choices to make about

_____

_____

As I recall past moves, I felt as though I was able to make important choices about

_____

_____

When I think about my/our next move, I feel as though I have few or no choices to make about

_____

_____

When I think about my/our next move, I look forward to making important choices about

_____

_____

EXERCISE B

Look at the list of nouns you chose to describe yourself in Chapter Two, particularly those you chose as the most important. What do you need to successfully carry out these roles? Be specific. For example, if your role as a figure skater is important to you, you need ice as well as access to a good coach, and a community in which figure skating is valued.

In order to be a _____, I'll need _____
_____
_____in my community.

In order to be a _____, I'll need _____
_____
_____in my community.

In order to be a _____, I'll need _____
_____
_____in my community.

In order to be a _____, I'll need _____
_____
_____in my community.

In order to be a _____, I'll need _____
_____
_____in my community.

EXERCISE C

Below we've listed some (not all) items movers often consider as they research a new community.

FIRST: Read through the entire list.

NEXT: Cross out the items on the list which are not important to you in a new community.

FINALLY: Complete the list by adding to it those things which you know you're hoping to find in a new community. Feel free to borrow ideas from the Lifescan you completed in Chapter Two.

- Housing
- Paid work for you (in your profession)
- Paid work for partner (in his/her profession)
- Opportunity for you to change field of work
- Opportunity for partner to change field of work
- Climate you enjoy
- Recreational centers
- Safety: environmental, personal
- Public transportation
- Child care
- Shopping
- Schools for children
- Schools for self and/or spouse/partner
- Proximity to family/friends
- Access to health services
- Others

_____

_____

_____

EXERCISE D

Now: Look again at the list you made in EXERCISE C. Pick from that list the five most important items and complete the following:

1. In order to get information about _____
   I will contact _____

2. In order to get information about _____
   I will contact _____

3. In order to get information about _____
   I will contact _____

4. In order to get information about _____
   I will contact _____

5. In order to get information about _____
   I will contact _____

EXERCISE E

For those of you who plan to visit the community you're thinking about moving to, use the following as a guide for gathering and recording information (you may want to write the headings into a notebook):

Preparing for the Visit
   During my visit, I'd like to gather information about

   _____

   _____

   _____

   _____

The people/places I want to see during my visit include

_____

_____

_____

_____

During the Visit

Here are some observations I'd like to record

_____

_____

_____

_____

Recalling the Visit

Here's what I liked about the community

_____

_____

_____

_____

Here's what I disliked about the community

_____

_____

_____

_____

I'd like more information about

_____

_____

_____

_____

_____

_____

CHAPTER 5

Now Make a Win-Win Decision

Now the countdown begins...

Your Lifescan has helped you know yourself better. You have explored a new community to learn whether its characteristics and yours would make a good fit. You are facing two decisions: whether to move, and where to go.

This is the time to gather the pieces into a choice that is respectful of your rights, needs, and wishes, and responsive to the rights, needs, and wishes of your loved ones. How might a choice like that look?

A COUPLE CHOOSES

Negotiation was the name of the game when Ellen and Ron decided to settle down after ten years of hopscotching around the country so that he could fulfill his dream of becoming an eye surgeon. They had married when Ron was in medical school, and three children were born during his years of further training. Ellen reared them as an almost-single parent as she followed her husband, making a home, dismantling a home, making friends, parting from friends, and trying to patch together a career of her own. Resourceful and optimistic, Ellen adjusted and re-adjusted. Then she hit the wall.

"After this, it's my turn to choose," she stormed to Ron soon after their move to the north. The geographic climate was bleak, the human climate felt cold. There were no jobs in her field of interior design, and Ellen's bottled-up resentment against Ron erupted.

Shaken up, he saw the fairness of Ellen's claim. Negotiations about their next move took place in a quiet cafe away from their humming household. They agreed that each would have veto power, and Ellen exercised it first when Ron proposed staying where they were. The rural setting, hiking, skiing, and mountaineering appealed to him a lot.

"No way! I need the pulse of big city life," Ellen protested. "I need pavement, not meadows." But too much pavement stifled Ron, so they compromised. A small city it would be, surrounded by countryside.

They scanned a map. With his nomadic spirit, Ron wanted the field of choice to include distant states. That didn't suit Ellen. After years of disruption, she needed familiarity—a small eastern city with professional opportunities for herself. And she longed for a place "where someone will claim me"—a family member or friend who would help gather the family into the new community.

Ron sought a medical group with an opening for an ophthalmologist. He wanted a group to have high ethical standards and commitment to *pro bono* service for patients without insurance.

Ellen wanted changing seasons, but a shorter winter. As the field narrowed, she compared two close contenders by looking at the chamber of commerce calendar, and noticing the date of the annual flower show. In one city, spring came two weeks sooner than the other.

As the couples' priorities fell into place, the search intensified. When the final choice was made, both felt well treated. Each had stood firm about some wishes, set others aside, and agreed about many. They felt a fresh clarity about themselves, and a zestful anticipation of starting a new life together.

Ellen and Ron's style of making a decision reflected their commitment to themselves, each other, and their children. Yet it had taken a major jolt to involve them that way—the realization that their relationship had been jeopardized by a decade of intense pressures, repeated relocation, and insufficiently examined choices.

Many people have trouble making choices that protect their own rights, needs, and wishes, yet respond to those of loved ones. Here are some obstacles that men and women each face.

MALE OBSTACLES

Jim, a geologist, approached his friend Max to talk over a job offer from a distant firm. He spoke of the opportunity for field work and his chances for promotion. He discussed the colleagues he would work with and the boss. He talked about his salary, retirement benefits, and "perks."

"How does Janet feel about moving?" Max asked, after an hour of listening. Jim looked startled. "My wife wants to live wherever I want to work—at least, I think she does." Jim hadn't, it seemed, probed Janet's reactions. Was Jim indifferent to his wife's needs? Max knew that wasn't so. But other influences were working here.

First, Jim had grown up in a traditional household, with a mother who devoted her life to her husband and sons. Jim married a woman who fit the same mold. He expected her to accept his goals as her own.

Second, Jim was making the widely-held assumption that families will follow the career trajectory of their men. It's an assumption partially shaped by need—a man must go where there's a job to be done. But it's shaped by a sense of entitlement, too. If a man is the chief financial provider for his family, he should be able to choose where to carry that out. Not all men recognize that their partners' roles as emotional and social providers have comparable importance.

Third, in seeking recognition for himself as an individual, Jim was doing what American society applauds males for doing from boyhood onward.

Seth, a photographer, came to Max three months later. He was content with his life, but his wife, a science professor, was not. Amidst competitive colleagues and with dwindling funds to support her research, Karen wanted to move to another university.

Karen's career had a high priority in Seth's life. Reluctant as he was to move, he would agree if he could find a good job for himself. He had broken with the tradition of the advancing male and the "trailing" wife. But for him as much as Jim, work was central in his decision-making.

"What other things are you searching for in a new place?" Max asked, and Seth looked puzzled. "I hadn't really thought much about it."

Even though new life choices are opening up for men—being house-husbands, for example—most men still define themselves by their paid work. That self-definition shapes their decision about moving, at least until retirement.

We've asked you, our male readers, to go beyond Seth and Jim and scan the whole fabric of your lives. You may think we are pulling you into murky realms, and there are good reasons for your reaction.

Boys growing up in America are rarely encouraged to be introspective. Rather, they are pressured to focus outward and to act rather than to reflect. They are encouraged to push aside their emotions, or release them, unexamined, through channels like competitive sports.

For those reasons, trying to fathom the feelings attached to places and relationships can be unsettling. It is tempting to short-circuit that sticky effort and focus only on the workplace. We hope you won't.

FEMALE OBSTACLES

It's considered more acceptable for women to be concerned with their emotions and relationships. Single women, or women paired with women, usually factor personal attachments into their decisions about moving.

The balance shifts for women paired with men. The needs of the male partner may prevail as women become mired in an I/We dilemma. We described it in Chapter 2; here again is what we mean.

From early childhood, a girl is encouraged to maintain connection—accepting care from others and giving it too. As she grows out of the cocoon of her family, she forms new relationships of intimacy—with a dear friend, a lover, a child of her own. She is likely to experience interludes of feeling merged with the other. The boundary between the self as an "I" and the self as a "we" can be blurred. When a major decision is made, the "I" can get lost in the "we."

"Choosing the law school that Alan would go to was a clear 'we' proposition," declared Sally, a twenty-three-year-old mover, whose story portrays the lost "I." Together, she and Alan investigated thirteen law schools, examining the programs, the costs, and the locations, before choosing the school that Alan would attend. "Together," they decided on a New England school.

Later, Sally said vehemently, "I hate the cold. It frightens me—I feel unsafe. I chill easily and I don't want to go out." From prior exposure to northern climates, she had known those things. She had simply ignored the fact that cold would pervade her life for three years.

Sally was a dental technician. She enjoyed her work, and expected to provide income while Alan was in school. But she also failed to factor her job prospects into the decision about moving. "I just assumed there would be jobs in my field. In Nashville, the newspapers were full of openings. I was stunned when I realized how hard it was to find a job and how low the salaries were here."

Sally was convinced the decision to move north was mutual, shared with her husband. Insofar as her decision reflected her commitment to help him reach his goal, it was a "we" decision, embracing his professional aim and her caregiving aim. Her aim was merged with his. But her "I" aims—feeling safely warm, having a satisfying job—were lost in the "we." Sally put her well-being at risk. The "I" of many coupled women movers is placed at risk in similar ways.

Some women are more comfortable than Sally in responding to their "I" aims. But, since women are expected, and expect themselves, to care for others, the "I" aims may feel selfish.

Martina, a twenty-nine-year-old wife and mother, agonized over a decision to apply to medical school. This would fulfill a childhood dream she had set aside to marry and have her own child—a choice her parents applauded. They now labeled her "selfish" for wanting to be a doctor, and their disapproval stirred Martina's guilt. She felt as selfish as they saw her.

Learning of her dreams of helping others by becoming a physician, a counselor questioned why the wish for medical training seemed selfish. Why would taking care of sick people be less altruistic than giving care to her husband and child?

It would be less altruistic, Martina explained, because she would have satisfactions in addition to healing. Looking ashamed, she confided her wish for the prestige that a medical degree would confer, as well as the power to influence health care decisions.

If the "I" aims of a coupled woman can be viewed as financial necessity—for example, if a second income is important to maintain a certain standard of living—they are accepted. Others will believe that her primary concern is with the needs of her family. But "I" aims concerned with personal recognition outside of the home are still cloaked in shame and guilt for many women, and arouse mistrust in onlookers. "I" wishes can cause such painful tension in a coupled woman mover that she will disregard them, as Sally did.

So the "I/we" dilemma impedes wise choices among women. But the interplay between helplessness and power also plays a role. Except for African-American women, who were rarely allowed this possibility, the ideal wife of the 1950s and '60s was self-effacing—sheltered by her husband's earnings, enhanced by his accomplishments, identified by his name, and nourished by his approval. In spite of the alternatives opened up for both men and women by the Women's Movement, many couples still accept this ideal.

"It never crossed my mind that I had a choice," said Andrea, a thirtysomething wife, who became deeply depressed after her seventh move (wine helped to fend it off until then). "My husband always made the decisions—he said, 'everyone moves this much,' and I believed him. I never had thoughts of not going with him. I do love him, and I've felt very dependent on him."

In their adulthood, wives like Andrea enter a state termed "learned helplessness." In that state, they disqualify themselves from decisions affecting their lives. Paradoxically, though, dependence and helplessness may be paralleled by a sense of power.

"I felt it was up to me to make it all work for the family," Andrea explained, and she is echoed by other wives who see themselves as the matrix of their families—sympathetic, comforting, and encouraging; skillful organizers who support their husbands and children in their occupational, educational, and social undertakings. They see themselves as able to absorb and heal their families' stresses and to respond wisely to their needs. Such women feel protective not only towards their children, but towards their husbands too, often seeing the men as less resilient, less adaptable than themselves.

This confidence in their nurturing power can lead such traditional wives to subscribe to the Myth of the Transportable Homemaker, which we've discussed in Chapter 2. This is a myth that disregards the web of supportive connections that enables a homemaker to find satisfaction in her role—support that enables her to tolerate the fragmentation, discontinuity, repetition, frustration, and isolation that seem inevitable in even the most fulfilling domestic life. It's a widely accepted myth that causes homemakers to believe, "I can do it anywhere," and to silence their voices when a decision about moving is made.

IMPEDIMENTS FOR COUPLES

Until recently, the tradition of virilocality prevailed. That is, where a married man went, his wife went too. Some states encoded the tradition in law. A wife who declined to move with her husband could be named as a deserter from the family, and would forfeit financial rights and sometimes parental rights as well.

Fewer couples accept that as a rightful tradition today. Yet it is deeply rooted. Even young couples committed to the idea of shared choice may unwittingly accept the assumptions embodied in that tradition: 1) a woman's fulfillment should be attained primarily through her man; 2) the role of a homemaker is readily transportable; 3) a woman's career can more easily be interrupted and resumed than a man's; 4) she is not fully entitled to meet her own needs.

Some women make a conscious choice to sacrifice their interests for the sake of their partner, imagining they will be rewarded down the line. Some men are now doing the same, especially to promote a partner's career. If the sacrifice is limited, both in time and degree, it can be a constructive expression of love. But if it extends too long, or is taken for granted, it can breed resentment in the sacrificer, and guilt in the partner.

More often than men, women avoid the discomfort of asserting their "I" wishes by handing over a decision about moving to male partners. Men still feel entitled to make the decision. But if he does, a man may accept more than he expects.

"Since it was Jim's career that was involved, I let him decide. It would be his responsibility if the move didn't work out for the family. Then I could blame him—and I would too!" This mover wryly highlighted the burden her husband had assumed. And she provided one answer to a crucial question: Why does it matter if the voice of one partner is silenced?

There are many reasons.

It matters because all people face stresses in life that are beyond their control. To maintain a sense of mastery, they need to make active choices whenever possible.

It matters because people who have abdicated choices lose dignity and feel victimized. Victimization breeds resentment, even rage. Resentment and rage seek a target. The most likely target is a loved one close at hand—spouse, lover, or even a child. Such targets respond with guilt, anger, anxiety, and relationships are eroded.

It matters because ill-considered choices compromise people's capacity for effective work and for love. Their pain will flow outward, affecting their intimates, their community, their world.

CONSTRUCTIVE STRATEGIES FOR ADULTS

Consider what people need when they face major decisions. It's surprisingly similar for adults and children. People need:

To feel included. Being included in a decision means that you're considered a significant person in your family or in your group.

To be informed. Having information reduces feelings of helplessness. Put another way, knowing is a way of feeling in charge.

To ask questions. Being informed isn't a one-time event. Strong feelings interfere with taking information in. You can only assimilate a little at once. You need to feel free to ask for more and more information over time, and even to repeat the same questions.

To have choices. You thrive when you feel in control of your life. Being able to make appropriate choices fosters that feeling.

To understand the limits. You need to know how much influence it's possible to have on a major decision.

To express a range of feelings. The prospect of major change usually kindles a variety of emotions. They may be contradictory and will probably vary over time. They need to be expressed.

To feel understood. Others may not share your feelings, but you need to have others listen and try to understand. You need others to accept your right to feel whatever you feel.

To feel stability. When major aspects of life are changing, you need to identity the realms that will provide a stable core. Those may be certain relationships, certain roles, or certain places.

To feel reassured. Major changes can be exciting, but they're often frightening too. You need to know that there are people available to help when you are lonely or scared.

As you progress toward making your decision, check back several times to see if those needs are being met. Be alert to choices that are easily overlooked. If there's clearly no choice about moving—because it's mandated by the military, for example—there may still be choices about where you will live and what kind of housing you will choose.

Most people think of making a decision as a reasoned weighing of pros and cons. It is that, but it's more. Conscious ideas are influenced by subconscious ones. Thoughts are influenced by emotions. To make a sound decision, you need to take into account the feelings, attitudes, daydreams, and memories that hover at the margins of your awareness.

Since all people wear blinders, it's difficult to do that alone. Whether you are a single mover, a coupled mover, or a family mover, it's wise to involve a trusted other person in the process of making a decision.

If you have a partner, you can help each other with your Lifescans and your study of the prospective community. You can meet regularly in a quiet and private place. There you can think through, feel through, and talk through your choices. If you have no partner, try to involve a close friend or relative the same way.

Couples may need the help of an outsider too—friend, relative, colleague, clergy person, or even a professional counselor. It should be someone who cares about you, and who will ask you challenging questions. That someone should ensure that both of your voices are heard.

If you and your partner are committed to reaching a decision that respects each other's rights, needs, and wishes, the process can deepen your understanding of each other and strengthen your relationship.

You can express your mutual care by looking at the gains of not moving as seriously as you look at the gains of moving. You can ask yourselves why a new vocational opportunity should take precedence over the personal connections that will be ruptured. You can think creatively about ways that life can be enriched by developing potentials within yourselves—new realms of learning, new roles, new relationships. Either psychological moves or geographic moves can be chosen. Or both.

DECIDING WITH YOUR CHILDREN

TAKE STOCK

Since communication is at the heart of decision-making, this is a fine time to take stock of your typical ways of communicating with your child. Do you spend a lot of time in conversation, or is it rare? Who's usually the talker? Who's the listener? What helps you have good conversation? What gets in the way?

This is a good time to take stock of how you and your child make decisions, from the everyday matters (What's for dinner? Can a friend come over to play?) to the big-time matters (Will my child attend private or public school? Should my child go to sleep away camp next summer? Is my child ready to start dating?) Do you make decisions in a democratic way, with your child having a lot of input? Do you make decisions in an autocratic way, making them for your child? Do you vary in your style? What usually works out best?

If you're moving with a partner, take stock of whether you agree or disagree about the role your children should have in making the decision. Try to reach some agreement, so that you don't give out confusing mixed messages, and so they don't play one of you against the other.

DECIDE

When is the best time to begin talking with your child about moving. Is it when the move is a mere possibility? Is it best to wait until you have to decide, or until the decision has been made? It's wise to strike a balance. Knowing about a major life change a year in advance can burden a child. Yet children readily sense when something big is up. Even if no adult conversation is overheard (it usually is), your facial expression, tone of voice, even the way you move will signal to your child your excitement, tension or fear. It worries children to sense that something important is going to happen when they don't understand what that "something" is.

Where can you talk with your child most effectively? It's hard for youngsters to follow an adult prescription to "sit down and talk it over." Keeping the body still and having eye contact can cause too much tension to build up. True, a young child may feel safest on your lap, although s/he may need to get down and move around to release the tension. With an older child, taking a walk together works well, since the movement allows tension to drain off, and intense eye contact can be avoided. Where have you had your most successful conversations with your child? Wherever you choose, try to open the conversation in a private place, since your child may have a sudden, intense, and loud reaction.

What part can your child play in making the decision? Few, if any, parents would expect their children to make the decision themselves. But does that mean that children's voices should be silenced? Within the choice about whether or not to move, other choices are included. Talks with your children, and a look at their Lifescans, can deepen your understanding of their needs. That may influence your decision.

When Gretchen was fourteen, her father was offered a prestigious position in a distant city. She was distraught at the thought of leaving her circle of close friends, leaving her favorite math teacher, leaving the school orchestra in which she was a valued flautist. Understanding that her need for attachment, identity, and stability (during the turbulence of adolescence) was greater than his own need for a new challenge, he decided to forego the opportunity until later in his life.

When Alvina was eleven, her mother was graduating from medical school and faced the question of where to apply for her residency training. Alvina was talented and committed to ballet, so her mother applied only to hospitals in cities with good ballet schools that would accept an African American student.

When Derek was seven, the decision about moving to a small city was out of his hands. But his wish for a home with a tree big enough for a tree house was seriously taken into account.

EXPLAIN

Explain to your children that you are thinking about moving. If you know, tell them when you'll be reaching a decision, or when the move will take place. Keep in mind that a young child's ideas of time are different than yours. You may need to anchor the "when" to some familiar event like swimming season or the start of school.

Explain what each family member's role will be in the decision-making process. Be clear about what your child's input does and does not include. For example, you might say: *"You get to ask questions, tell me anything you think or feel or wonder or worry about. You get to be happy or mad, or both. You get to give me all your ideas. I get to listen to you, talk with you, think about all the things you've told me, and then it will be time for me to make the decision about moving. I'll need a lot of help from you so I can make a really good decision. Then I can help you understand why I made the decision, and what will happen."*

Try to keep the first one or two conversations about moving brief and simple. This can be a big, scary, confusing idea for a young child to grasp. There will be plenty of time later to talk more.

WAIT

Children need time to think about things adults tell them, especially something as significant as a move. Don't be surprised or disappointed if your child does not react instantly. S/he may need a break, and will want to play, or to go off alone to think about what you have discussed. Or your timing may have been off—you may have brought up the subject five minutes before your child's favorite TV show began.

Give your child time to absorb the idea of moving, and give yourself time to reflect about his/her initial reactions (they may have upset you). You'll be talking more about those later.

Expect unpredictability. One day your children may express enthusiasm for a move, but a few days later they may be totally opposed. This is common. Your children are experimenting with their feelings, and probably feel a range of emotions.

LISTEN

This may be hard. Your child may express fear, worry, or refusal to consider a move, and those reactions may churn up your own troubled feelings. But try to convey that it's OK to vent feelings and to ask a lot of questions. If questions aren't voiced, maybe your tone of voice or facial expression signals that it's really not OK. You may need to admit that the idea of moving bothers you, too, but that it's important to keep asking and talking.

Try to listen a little more carefully than usual when your children play. Their feelings are often expressed in imaginative play with dolls, trucks, action figures, and other toys.

If your child attends day care or school, or is cared for by another adult in your home, let teachers and caregivers know that you are talking about moving. Ask them to let you know if they notice any behavior that may be related to moving.

ACCEPT

The best thing you can do now is to try to listen sympathetically to all the feelings your children express about moving, even contradictory ones. This is hard if it stirs up your own sadness or anxiety—you may need to turn to the adults who are supporting you.

Try to validate your children's feelings rather than simply reacting. This will be difficult, too, especially if their feelings are the opposite of your own. But it will help them feel understood, and will foster the use of words rather than behavior to express negative reactions. And it may help your children assimilate the information you'll be giving.

Here are examples of parent's responses that validate:
- "It sounds like you would be sad if we decide to move."
- "It sound as though you'd like to live in a different place."

Here are example of responses that do not validate:
- "You're just being silly when you say that."
- "How can you possibly know that you don't want to move?"

A wide range of feelings can be accepted, but undesirable behavior cannot. You may have to set limits, helping your children see the difference between feeling angry, or saying they're angry—both OK—and behaving angrily by stomping your eyeglasses into the ground.

REASSURE

Even the most secure child can become overwhelmed, confused, and frightened at the thought of change, loss, and the unfamiliar. No matter how much support and understanding you convey in your conversations about moving, it is likely that your children will feel anxious.

This doesn't mean that you shouldn't talk about moving (or that you should never move!). It does mean that your children need reassurance that they will be well taken care of. It is important to be both honest and reassuring at the same time.

For example: "I don't know yet whether we will be moving, but I do know that we will be OK together no matter where we decide to live." But do avoid making promises you may not be able to keep.

OBSERVE

Be alert to changes in your child's play or general behavior since you began talking about moving. Try to initiate a conversation about what you've noticed. For example: "You seem kind of sad tonight. Are you thinking about moving, or is there something else on your mind?"

Observe yourself also. Have you been talking about moving with a friend or partner in front of your children? Is it wise to do that? How much information are your children absorbing indirectly? Is it helping them or hurting?

REPEAT

All of the steps we have described, except for *Decide*, are equally important, and don't need to be carried out in a special sequence. Each will tend to be repeated, perhaps many times.

If the children realistically have no choice about whether to move, there are many choices they can have. They may help choose the kind of neighborhood and home you'll live in, the kind of school to go to, or the kind of recreational facility to look for. They can have choices in the decision-making process, such as when you'll talk about the move, how many questions each gets to ask, who gets to talk first.

Encouraging your children to weigh their own gains and losses allows them to take an active role in the decision-making process too. Even if their wants don't ultimately affect your decision, helping them think (and feel) about the gains and losses they face will help to prepare them for the exciting experience to come.

Chapter 5 Exercises

You've been reading about different styles of decision making, and the eventual impact those styles can have on movers. You've read about individuals who let their partner make all or most of the decisions about a move, as well as couples who learned to make fair and responsible choices based on a lot of talking, listening, and compromising.

What is your style? The following exercise will challenge you to look closely at ways in which you typically make decisions, and to think about how you'd like to participate in the decisions about your next move.

EXERCISE A

Think of someone you know who has recently moved. Ask that person:

How did you make your decision?

_____
_____
_____

What was your role in the final decision to move?

_____
_____
_____

In what ways (if any) would you change the way you made this recent decision about moving?

_____
_____
_____

EXERCISE B

Now think about the last major decision you made—for example, to rent or buy a home, to accept a new job, to return to school, to become a stay-at-home parent.

Describe how you made that decision:

_____

_____

Who else was part of the decision, and what was his/her role?

_____

_____

What was your role?

_____

_____

Did you feel that you talked enough? too much? not enough?

_____

_____

Did you or your partner exercise veto power? _____

What was the impact of exercising veto power?

_____

_____

Would you make that decision in the same way today? __
If not, how would you make that decision differently?

_____

_____

EXERCISE C

As you move toward a decision about moving, ask yourself:
In what ways are you and your partner and/or children sharing the decision together?

_____

_____

What do you like so far about the ways in which you're approaching your decision?

_____

_____

What do you dislike, or feel is unfair or uncomfortable so far?

_____

_____

_____

EXERCISE D

Complete these statements to sort out how you feel about deciding:
The hardest part about this process of deciding is

_____

_____

The part I enjoy about the process of deciding is

_____

_____

I wish my partner would

_____

_____

I wish my partner would not

_____

_____

EXERCISE E

Think about your coming move.

How do you think your partner and/or child would describe
how you feel about moving?

_____

_____

_____

Describe how your partner and/or child feels about moving.

_____

_____

_____

EXERCISE F

If not moving is a choice you are considering:

What are the losses?

_____

_____

_____

What are the gains?

_____

_____

_____

SECTION TWO

On Your Mark, Get Set...

No your daddy and I aren't divorced. We're just enduring a transient employment-related unilateral geographic dislocation.

CHAPTER 6

Set Your Dates: "If" Becomes "When"

So you have decided to move. When will it happen? If the semester is beginning at your college, if the lease on your apartment can't be renewed, if your employer is transferring you, the date may be out of your control. Or so it may seem.

People who have a sense of choice about moving tend to adapt more comfortably than those who feel forced. So consider what aspects of the timing you could control. Might your landlady give you an extension? Could you negotiate the starting date with your new employer? You may have more influence than you suppose.

🏠

If you do have leeway in setting your date, turn back to your Lifescan. Think about all the involvements that give you satisfaction in your life. Ask yourself when it will be easiest to leave them. It may be easiest if you can leave without feeling you are letting others down. And it may be easiest when you have a sense of closure—when a project is finished, or when the season for a particular activity has past.

Every member of the family may want some input here. Your mother-in-law may long to celebrate one more Hanukkah together. Your son may plead for one more birthday party with his buddies.

Finding the least wrenching time for your departure is one side of the coin. The other side is considering when the new community may be most receptive to newcomers. In what season are people most likely to be sauntering around town, or gathering in cafes, playgrounds or parks? In what season are they likely to be invisible—cloistered in air-conditioned buildings, or scurrying through the cold in a cocoon of clothing? What time of year does your new workplace or community have welcoming events for newcomers—picnics, potlucks, or receptions? If you didn't find out when you were researching the new community, this is the time to ask.

Families with school-aged children may believe that a move should be postponed until summer vacation. There are benefits to that. During the summer, you could explore the new community together. Your children may enroll in summer programs that let them start making new friends. Yet there may be a dark side to a summertime move. Some communities empty out in the summer. Mothers and children may go to beach cottages or mountain cabins, while fathers commute on week-ends. Moving into a suburb without summer playmates would be bleak for the children and frustrating for parents wanting to establish their own networks. So add Summer Exodus onto your list of things to ask about in advance.

More things to think about: If you move after school has started, tight groups may have already formed among the youngsters, and your children may have trouble working their way in. But there's a sunny side. A child who enters a new school during the year can be the focus of helpful, special attention. In Chapters 9 and 10 we suggest ways to help with the transition.

SEPARATE DATES FOR DIFFERENT FAMILY MEMBERS

A moving date that is best for one family member may be disruptive for another. The whole family may not need to move at once.

PARTNERS MOVING AT SEPARATE TIMES

"For me, it was as simple as getting off one train and onto another," said Ben as he recalled his moves from one engineering firm to another. But for his wife, those "simple" transitions were intensely stressful. She stayed behind and carried out the social, emotional, and practical work of moving the household.

If your partner is moving on a designated date, how may you feel about waiting until later? You may feel burdened by the tasks of moving. You may resent the lack of support from your absent partner, and resentment corrodes relationships. And if your partner moves as Ben did, emotionally uninvolved in the process, s/he won't understand what you are living through alone. That, too, will fray the bonds of affection.

There's another thing to consider. The partner who goes first may not move as smoothly as Ben did. S/he may feel lonely, anxious, and—at moments—abandoned by the one who stayed behind.

On the other hand, deciding to move after your partner could increase your feeling of being in charge of your life. A delay may allow you to wind up your own work. It may help bridge the period when your partner is so engrossed in the new job that s/he wouldn't be very available to you anyway.

But it will be a constructive bridge only under certain conditions: If you feel well supported by family or friends where you are now; if you feel comfortable asking for the help you need; if you work out an agreement with your partner about how the practical tasks of moving will be shared; and if you plan ways to stay positively connected.

"The phone, of course," you're probably thinking. The phone is a powerful instrument of connection—and disconnection, too. That is, although you'll reach for the phone to share your highs, you'll want to share your lows as well. It's painful for separated partners to hear each other's worries and disappointments when there's so little opportunity to be helpful. One partner may feel guilty for letting the other down. Or if resentment and anger come through on the phone, that can cause a breach that's difficult to repair at a distance. Too, since you can't read each other's faces on the phone, there's more risk of misunderstandings.

If you have to move at different times, each of you will need to let off steam to a confidante, so that your conversations with each other won't be unbearably intense. And when you are reunited, there will be a tense period of readjustment to each other, and this will coincide with the inevitable stresses of moving. You will both need support.

For children, parental separation may be worrisome. They will need repeated reassurance that your separation is different from the divorces they hear about from their friends. They will need to stay connected with the absent parent through phone calls, taped messages, postcards, photos, and specially chosen gifts. Even so, they will miss the absent parent, and may react with troublesome behavior. It helps to be prepared for that.

CHILDREN MOVING AT SEPARATE TIMES

When the Brown family moved to Oregon, Granger and the two older children moved first. His wife, Pip, and the four younger children followed four months later, after their California home was sold. Granger arranged to work a lighter than normal schedule until Pip joined him, in order to be a househusband as well as a dentist. For him, that interlude of extra involvement with his youngsters was a special time.

"We still talk about it," he said years later. "The kids joke about some of the strange things I cooked, but the way they joke about it makes me think it was pretty special for them, too."

In that family, the older children moved first. It often works well the other way around. If you have teen-aged children, it may be a hardship for them if the family moves during the school year, or in the summer before their last year of high school (see Chapter 3). You all need to put your heads together to find a creative solution. Here are some examples.

Alicia, a CPA, was frustrated by the policies in her firm, and hoped to find another position. Her husband, Joel, was open to a change. As a high school math teacher, he felt optimistic about finding a job almost anywhere she wanted to go. When Alicia was offered a post in a town two hours away, it seemed a good time for a family move.

Peter, who would be starting in junior high, and changing schools anyway, seemed to accept the idea. But Robert, who was about to begin his senior year and was captain of the wrestling team, was very upset. "It's the pits," he grumbled to Alex, his closest friend. Alex, who didn't want Robert to leave either, put the problem to his parents. "Couldn't Robert live with us? He could share my room."

That turned out to be the solution. Robert's parents paid board for their son, and planned to visit on week-ends, especially when Robert had wrestling matches. On other week-ends, Robert would take the bus and visit his family in their new home.

When Win, a banker, was told he was being laid off, he searched hard for a job near home. The closest he could find was four hours away. After many long family discussions, this was decided: Win would move with their fourteen-year-old son, who would be starting high school. Diana would stay behind with their daughter, a high school senior, until after her graduation. In that interlude, Diana could finish a work project of her own.

It was a year of comings and goings, with family reunions alternating between one town and the other. But hectic as it was, all the members knew that they had tried their best to meet everyone's needs and wants.

Doug's family found still another solution. When his father was offered a fine job one and a half hours from their home, Doug, too, was in his senior year at school. This family decided to postpone moving until after graduation, even though the three-hour daily commute was arduous for Doug's father.

For Dwayne, the decision to stay put while he finished high school had an unhappy outcome. Dwayne's parents were divorcing, and each planned to move to a new town. Rather than go with either one, Dwayne chose to stay with his older brother, who lived and worked in their home town.

Perhaps his parents didn't know, or didn't take seriously, the fact that the brother was a heavy drinker who let Dwayne have too free a rein. Dwayne began cutting classes and dealing drugs—in fact, his slide into trouble was so deep that he needed months of help in a residential treatment center before he could get his young life together again.

Dwayne had clearly been overloaded by the loss of his home and the loss of his parents, and a young adult brother who couldn't handle the responsibility. Dwayne had reason to feel unvalued and abandoned. In each of the other instances, the youngster who stayed behind to finish school had one or more concerned and responsible adults right on the scene.

For a single parent who needs to move ahead of a youngster, it can be crucial to find relatives or friends who will take your youngster in and make a commitment to his or her care. Even then, it's important to plan with your youngster when you'll visit and how you'll stay in touch during the lonely times between visits.

Almost any date you choose will have pros and cons. The date will be important, but the way in which you decide will matter just as much. You might review our guidelines for constructive decision making (Chapter 5), since this is an opportunity to convey to your loved ones that you respect their rights and value their viewpoints.

Chapter 6 Exercises

EXERCISE A

As you set your moving date, you may realize that not everyone in your family will be able (or will choose) to move together. Here are some issues for you to think about and then discuss with other family members.

If I move first, without my partner or family...
I'd be doing that because

_____

_____

I'd be responsible for

_____

_____

I'd worry about

_____

_____

I might enjoy

_____

_____

I'd need help with

_____

_____

I'd also need

_____

_____

I'd stay connected with my family by

_____

_____

I'd take care of myself by

_____

_____

I'd count on and need my family to

_____

_____

I think I could live separately until

_____

_____

If my partner or family moves first and I stay behind...
I'd be doing that because

_____

_____

I'd be responsible for

_____

_____

I'd worry about

_____

_____

I might enjoy

_____

_____

I'd need help with

_____

_____

I'd also need

_____

_____

I'd stay connected with my partner/family by

_____

_____

I'd take care of myself by

_____

_____

I'd count on and need my partner/family to

_____

_____

I think I could live separately until

_____

_____

CHAPTER 7

Saying Good-Bye: Be Prepared for Surprises

AN EXCERPT FROM SYLVIA'S JOURNAL

Wrenching loose began on the day my husband accepted a challenging position in the north. When we had first considered the move, we tried to view our lives objectively. The inconveniences, frustrations, actual dangers (I had been mugged twice within a year) came into sharp focus. It seemed the right time to go.

But later, facing the reality of leaving, I felt an unbearable sense of ripping apart our lives. I felt surges of loathing for this man who seemed to be the cause—although I had agreed to the move. It is bleak to loathe your beloved—it is as though a sustaining warmth has been extinguished.

His own pain began to mount. At first, he was bewildered at the maelstrom that had seized me, and then he felt a heavy responsibility. His own impending losses came into focus. Doubts about his choice began to form.

So, now stoically, now in dull misery, now with sharp protest, we began the severance. We feared that our house would never be sold and feared that it would; endured strangers tramping through and gazing critically at the expressions of our innermost selves.

Our home was sold. We would vacate it just before the New Year began.

Too soon, it was Christmas Eve, the house flooded with carols, my family carrying out their secret rituals. I remembered the calm voice of a Swedish friend "If you see your move as the ending of your old life, you can only mourn. You could see it as the start of an exciting new one. Some people would give their right arm for that."

True. The move would be a beginning—an adventure of exploring and discovering anew that the capacity to be fulfilled is transportable within ourselves. But it was an ending too.

Christmas, a warmly shared time, was over. Ahead lay four dreaded days of final sorting, sifting, discarding, remembering, as we struggled with the detritus of twenty-seven years of family life.

In my generation, women were idealized as the matrix in a family—a glowing hearth to which each member could come for comfort. But how could I warm my husband, daughter, and son when I felt so cold?

Now it was December 26th. As I saw our faces, paled by fatigue, with darkly circled eyes and grim lines of strain, I wondered how the severance could be accomplished. We had cluttered our physical spaces with possessions; we had cluttered our spirits. Every object revived memories and a surge of longing for times past, or a wave of joy, or a shaft of pain.

December 27th. When defenses are frayed, the demons get loose. In the most loving family, there are seeds of hate. We shrieked accusations and protests, and if my husband and I avoided each other's glance, that was a sign of how desperate we felt, stabbed by doubt about our choice.

December 28th. Exhaustion dulls awareness. If I had fully realized what was happening that day, I would have felt raped. Our home was invaded by indifferent strangers who, deftly and swiftly, boxed and tied and hauled away those things that embodied our personal history. Each room was stripped naked, and five men tramped in and out of our private spaces. We kept seeking a refuge and instantly the cadre charged in on its remorseless quest. I wanted to shriek "Get out, get out!"

Then they were gone. We wandered from room to room to say good-bye to memories of voices and music and sights and smells and touch.

December 29th. This was The Day. Our station wagon, destined to transport necessities for the night before the van arrived, had expressed the family mood and broken down. A replacement part was sent from a distant city. It did not arrive. The van left. Our daughter and son left. Our dog left. Word came: the part was lost in transit. Our wagon would not go north.

We swept our house so that we could leave it proudly and crammed our paraphernalia into our smaller car. My husband took the wheel while I curled among mattresses and blankets and pans and food. Then, in the depth of night, we drove away.

Will your leaving be as wrenching as Sylvia's? Maybe yes, maybe no. Her attachments to her home and community were long-standing, widespread, and deep. Her reconnection—yes, it did happen—came slowly. But you, too, will go through many good-byes.

Good-byes are often welcome. Separating from an abusive partner, nosy neighbors, a supercritical teacher, a boring job, polluted air, roaring traffic, street crime, or poor schools can be cause for celebration. Those may be reasons why you decided to move. But it's a rare mover whose good-byes aren't also laced with sadness.

GOOD-BYE TO SPECIAL PEOPLE.

"My greatest fear is of being nobody, having no one close to me," said Emily, as she faced an unwanted move initiated by her ambitious husband. Close friendships sustained her where she was living. Like many women movers, she named separation from intimate friends as the most grievous loss of moving.

There are differences between male and female friendships (see Chapter 2). Both may be based on shared values and interests, on trust, genuine concern, and reciprocity. But male friendships are likely to be companionable, involving shared doing. Female friendships are more likely to be emotionally intimate, involving shared confiding. Friendship between women may be intense. Its flow of affection assures best friends that they are each lovable and loving. Its flow of understanding assures them that they are not alone. Loss of best friends can stir such pain that some movers compare it to bereavement.

Best friends may be the most difficult people to leave. But in doing your Lifescan you have noticed how many others are significant in your life: relatives, neighbors, colleagues, teachers, clergy, doctors, nurses, and hairdressers. Many of these are people who have taken care of you in some important way. As moving day draws closer, you may want to cling more tightly than before.

GOOD-BYE TO SPECIAL PLACES.

Jason and his partner, Mark, involved in the counterculture movement of the 1970s, lived in rural New England. They lived among young people who were turning away from a chaotic world, trying to affirm their self-sufficiency, creativity, and power to shape their own destinies. They were setting about it with saw, hammer and nail.

"We built our own house—I mean, physically built it ourselves," said Jason. "Every detail was just the way we wanted it—it was really an expression of who we both are. And we had a lot of privacy to be ourselves. When we had to move, the house was the hardest thing to leave."

Among the joys of my Connecticut life, there was a small class in creative movement, Sylvia wrote in her journal. *It was spontaneous, expressive. One autumn morning I went to class for the last time before our move. The air was soft and moist, holding the memory of summer's torpor. The others had already gathered in the plain room, with its white walls and wooden floor polished by bare feet. Our instructor started the music, and as the space filled with the haunting tones of Johann Pachelbel's Kanon in D, we turned our consciousness inward and allowed our bodies to move in a rhythmic meditation. I found myself bathed in melancholy, literally bathed. Tears poured down my face and over my neck and soaked my leotard. And then I was enfolded in the arms of comforting women. Without words, we said good-bye. That was ten years ago. If I hear Pachelbel even now, the tears well up again. Yet I wouldn't want that memory to dim, because the class was such a precious part of my life.*

That simple room was special to Sylvia as the locus of discoveries about her body in motion, and about emotions that the movements stirred. Too, it was the setting in which warm relationships with other women had grown. Your special places may have included other people, or they may have been retreats that you enjoyed in solitude. They may have been places where you had an exhilarating awareness of nature—maybe a beach by the pounding surf—or a calming realization of your small part in the universe.

If you completed your Lifescan, you know about those places. But as you visit them for the last time, It may surprise you to realize how complex your ties to those places are, and how reluctant you feel to leave them.

GOOD-BYE TO SPECIAL THINGS.

Your library, realtor, or van line can supply you with guides to physically efficient packing. But unless you wall off your emotions—not a wise idea, for reasons we'll discuss—the process won't be emotionally efficient.

"I hadn't realized how much 'things' meant to me until I had to start making choices," said Jennifer, who moved reluctantly at seventy-nine. "We couldn't take everything. Some things, the oriental rug, the dining room table, had been part of the family for so very long." Her eyes misted. "We had a huge world map up on the wall and each time a family member would take a trip we'd stick a pin in it to commemorate the journey. We didn't have space for that in our condominium."

"My husband was even more disturbed by the packing up than I was," said twenty-two-year-old Terry. "Ralph couldn't sort through things associated with his family—he'd get immobilized. I'd find him reading an old letter and crying. So I had to take over."

Most movers have to divest themselves of possessions. Many have limited funds for transporting possessions, or are moving into smaller living quarters, or simply welcome the chance to make a fresh start. It can feel good to de-clutter your life, and a yard sale can help the budget. But the divestment can feel exquisitely painful. Leaving behind a rocking chair in which you soothed your baby, a rusty tricycle, your high-school report cards—whatever embodies special memories and experiences—can feel like amputation. It is the loss of a segment of family continuity, of personal history. It's the loss of a part of your self.

Giving furniture or books or pictures to relatives or friends assuages the sense of loss. You can imagine the special chair and the special friend in a satisfying relationship. Your connection with the chair is preserved through the friend, your connection with the friend is preserved through the chair. But nonetheless, at the moment of giving, there is likely to be a jab of pain.

GRIEVING

From the first moment when you realize that your future won't include all those special people, places, and things, a process of grieving will be set in motion, and it can be intense. It may take you by surprise, especially if you are happy about making your move. In fact, you may mistakenly suppose that there's something wrong with you. Yet you should be more concerned if you don't grieve than if you do. Here's why.

Grief is more than a simple emotion; it's a complex psychological state. It includes sadness and longing, and often anger too—anger at the person or circumstance causing a loss. It's different from depression. The grieving person feels sad and deprived but not worthless or empty as the depressed person does. Put another way, grief is a state of sadness provoked by loss; depression is a state of diminished self-esteem provoked by failure. But if you're unprepared for your grief, and interpret it as a shameful sign of inadequacy, that may help tip you into depression.

At first, there may be anticipatory grief—sadness at the prospect of loss, and longing to hold onto what you're about to lose. Later, there may be sadness and longing to recapture what you did lose. Long-ago losses may come back into your thoughts and old sorrows may well up. Grief in the present often rekindles grief from the past.

There's more. The places and things you are leaving won't reproach you, but some of the people may. The one who moves is, in truth, abandoning those who stay behind. People who care a lot about you are likely to rejoice if your move is a positive one, but they will be sad and resentful, too. As one mover put it, "Our friends wined us and dined us, and said 'How can you do this to us?'"

Grief is pain and it's natural to want to avoid it. Some people try to cushion themselves against it by deliberately turning their thoughts away from impending losses. Some try to reason it away, reminding themselves that the places and people they are leaving will themselves change or move away.

For others, the surge of activity—sorting, packing, and dismantling their homes; negotiating with truckers and realtors; closing bank accounts, charge accounts, trash pick-ups; changing postal addresses and magazine subscriptions; attending farewell parties—can stimulate an emotional "high" (especially if they want to move), and mask grief about impending loss.

Some people separate their emotions from their thoughts and actions. Tina did that, at least for a while.

"I was like a zombie. I felt nothing much at all about moving. I was absorbed in closing down my business and the children. Then the day before the van came with the packers, my husband told me to choose the clothes I'd need for my cross-country drive. I went to the closet and stared at the clothes, and I was immobilized. I couldn't even think. Then I suddenly started to cry and I cried for two and a half hours, and I yelled and screamed. I told him to go alone, I and the children would stay behind. No, I didn't want to leave."

Sustained grief would be unbearable. The various defenses against its onslaught that we've just described are helpful if they allow the movers to remain organized and effective. The defenses are helpful if they allow the intensity of grief to ebb and flow.

But grieving is necessary work. Good cheer in the face of loss is often labeled courage and applauded, but it may not foster emotional health. Those who wall off their grief become vulnerable. There may be an explosive eruption such as Tina's and, if the mover is unprepared, s/he may feel ashamed or frightened. Or unacknowledged grief will express itself in indirect ways. Later, there may be mysterious depressions, unusual physical illnesses, or continuing emotional numbness.

Grieving is a constructive process. It allows you to let go of the real-life person, place, or thing, even as you store in your memory the images of that person, place, or thing, and thus keep them alive within yourself. It helps you adapt to loss and change.

STRATEGIES OF GRIEVING

It's wise to allow yourself to feel your sadness by going through rituals of good-bye. Visit the special places, have good-bye parties with the special people. The tears may flow, but they are healing tears.

When the sadness wells up, seek comfort for yourself. This is the time to claim the soothing you need. Consider what helps you feel cozy and safe. Is it a hot bath, a cup of herb tea, a professional massage? What helps invoke comforting images? Is it special music, a well-read book, the voice of an old friend on the phone? Once you have identified the sources of comfort, claim them! Let your partner, your parents and siblings, your friends know exactly what you need to survive this stressful time.

Grief often includes some apprehension and anger. This is a time for regular physical release—long, rhythmical swims or walks, biking, running, dancing, smashing a tennis ball, hurling a snow ball. The tension of fear and anger can flow out, with pleasure as a side-effect.

You need to feel understood and supported. This is the time to turn to a confidante to talk out all your troubled feelings about the move. It may be your closest friend, your minister or rabbi, a colleague, or a family member. When your confidante is not available, it may help to keep a journal, as Sylvia did.

Keep lines of communication open in your family so that your sadness can draw you together rather than apart. Use some of the communication strategies we discussed in Chapter 5. But keep in mind that your feelings and those of your loved ones are likely to follow different rhythms. One may feel upbeat and excited while another is scared and blue. You may be tempted to disqualify each other's feelings and try to convince each other that yours are "right." That isn't helpful. Rather, remember that each of you will feel a range of emotions at different times, and they need to be accepted.

And keep reminding yourself that your move is a beginning as well as an ending. If you build some bridges into your new life, the beginning will feel more real.

Chapter 7 Exercises

As you have read, grieving, although painful, allows you to adapt to loss and change. Planning ways to say good-bye to special people and places will help you feel and express the sadness, anger, and longing that are natural parts of grief.

EXERCISE A

Complete the following statements. Then share your responses with your partner and other family members.

As I prepare to move, I feel sad about

_____

_____

As I prepare to move, I feel angry about

_____

_____

_____

As I prepare to move, I long for

_____

_____

_____

The friends I'll miss intensely are

_____

_____

_____

The places I'll miss intensely are

_____

_____

_____

EXERCISE B

Think about how you want to say good-bye to people (start this soon, since life gets hectic as you approach moving day). With some, you'll want private time together, and may make specific plans to visit each other after the move. With others, you may want to say good-bye at a gathering, or send an informal note, or just mention that you are moving and you'll miss them. If you find lists helpful, why not jot down people's names and how you prefer to say good-bye to each one? It is important to let others know you are moving, so that they'll know why they don't see you any more.

Think about your closest friends. Try to arrange a time to meet with each one to show him/her your responses to exercise B.

Now ask your friends to complete these statements:
As I watch you prepare to move, I feel sad about

_____

_____

_____

As I watch you prepare to move I feel angry about

_____

_____

_____

As I watch you prepare to move, I long for

_____

_____

_____

EXERCISE D

Make time to visit places that are special to you. Draw sketches, make notes, or take pictures to help you remember the details.

CHAPTER 8

Building Bridges from Here to There

FINDING A SPONSOR

When Ellen and Ron decided to move (Chapter 5), Ellen wanted to find a place "where someone will claim me." She needed a relative or friend who would care about her and her family, and actively welcome them.

Movers who have someone who can act as an informal sponsor make their transitions more comfortably than those who don't. A sponsor can provide a warm welcome, offer companionship, introduce newcomers to people with similar interests, inform them about goods and services, and help them understand the customs and expectations of the community.

Who might serve as a sponsor? Relatives or friends already living in the new community may be ideal. Or you may have met helpful people while you were visiting. If you don't have such contacts, try to find one as you prepare for your move.

Ask your friends if they know people in the area. Gather names through your school or college alumni/ae association, your church, or the business or professional association you belong to. The chamber of commerce or a realtor should know if there's a Newcomer's Club or Welcome Wagon you could contact. If you or your partner are starting a new job, there may be a relocation office or a network of people eager to be helpful. If you are a college or postgraduate student, there are student or faculty advisors. The local newspaper may have a Letters column through which people can make contacts or gather information. You may tap into a source on Internet.

It may feel embarrassing to admit that you need support. But if you can accept the fact that moving—wanted or not—is highly stressful, and that it's appropriate for every mover to ask for help, you are likely to find people who will be happy to respond. It's good strategy to write notes to some whose names you've been given, identifying yourself as a soon-to-be-newcomer, and ask if they'd be willing to have you phone and draw on their knowledge of the community.

UNDERSTANDING THE NEW CULTURE

If you were moving (or even planning a trip) to a foreign country, you would probably try to familiarize yourself with its culture. You might study its language, read its history, learn about its beliefs and customs.

Since there are symbols of sameness found all over the USA—hamburgers, blue jeans, shopping malls—it's easy to overlook the differences. Yet every region, every community, every neighborhood has its own culture. It has a shared history, shared values, shared traditions, shared ways of looking at life. There may be certain hairstyles, styles of clothing, and even styles of speech that are emblems of belonging. There may be preferred foods and leisure time activities. There may be dominant political or religious beliefs.

Ellen, in her many moves with Ron, became aware that T-shirts are important emblems for children. Living on a southern military base, the children sported Mutant Ninja Rurtles. But when Ellen scouted the playgrounds in a rural northern community, there wasn't a turtle to be seen. She sensed that the violent ideas expressed by the turtles were unacceptable there, so she worked out a strategy with her children. After their move, they would wear dinosaurs in public for a while, and enjoy their turtles at bedtime.

You can follow Ellen's helpful example. When you visit your chosen community, it will be useful to take notes and photos to remind you how people look, and how they behave in public (notice the suggestions we've made in Chapter 4). But there's a lot that's unseen too.

When Jenny and Phil prepared to move, they focused on finding an affordable home on a safe cul-de-sac. They overlooked the culture of the neighborhood they chose. After they were settled in, Jenny realized it was not a good fit.

"Before I had kids, I worked on a newspaper," Jenny explained. "The neighborhood wasn't the center of my life. But, as a stay-at-home mom, I thought 'why wouldn't we all get together?' That's how I grew up—all the kids went out and played together. So I reached out to the women and said, 'hey, let's get together to do this or that,' but they didn't respond. I realized that we had important differences in philosophy about kids, and all sorts of different values. When I would run into them, they would ask me what I was doing this year, and I'd say I was writing articles. They seemed mystified. They go out selling Avon and Tupperware and Mary Kay, and here I am at home sitting at the computer. They don't know how to relate to me."

The husbands, although helpful and kind, were blue-collar workers who looked on professor Phil with misgivings. Their politics, their whole way of seeing the world, were different from Jenny and Phil's, and the couple soon felt awkward, lonely, and out of place.

"The neighbors know this is like a stopping ground for us, we're not going to live here forever," Jenny went on, targeting another feature of a neighborhood that should be explored. If a neighborhood is a settled one, the residents may be wary of those they view as transients.

"Peter and I befriended a number of newcomers," a long-settled New Englander explained. "But then, one by one, they moved on and left us, and we felt awful. So we decided we wouldn't risk that any more"

If you are making a long-term move, a settled neighborhood may be exactly what you want. But if your stay will be for fewer than four or five years, you may feel more supported in a neighborhood with a high proportion of newcomers.

Few people feel comfortable at the margin of a tightly bonded group of people who share racial, religious, or other ethnic characteristics. You may want to be a pioneer. You may have the courage and conviction to be the first African American in a Caucasian neighborhood. But keep in mind that just being a newcomer already puts you at the margin. Don't set yourself up for an overload.

As you continue to familiarize yourself with the culture of your chosen community, try to find out about its "initiation" customs. In the United States of America, there used to be rituals of welcome—calling on a newcomer, bringing food. By the middle of the 20th century, these began to disappear. They still exist in some areas, but not in many.

It will ease your transition if you find out in advance what is expected. Do the residents like to make welcoming gestures towards the newcomer? Should the newcomer take the initiative, or will the residents view that as being "pushy"? If the residents like to reach out, will that happen on an individual basis? Are there community events—maybe a picnic or pot-luck supper—planned for newcomers? Ask the person acting as your sponsor, and if s/he doesn't have the answers, ask that person to help you find out. Ask your realtor to help you gather information about neighborhoods you're interested in.

PLANNING CONTINUITIES

"The way my hair looks is absolutely central to my appearance," said a mover who worried about risking an unknown hairdresser in her new town. "If it's cut wrong, it takes so long to grow out, so long to repair." Many women movers travel back—sometimes a long distance—to their hairdressers in their former communities. Believing that their hairstyle is an important aspect of their physical identity, they need to hold on to that continuity as they go though the complex changes of relocation.

There is another reason, too. There are few ways in which an adult American woman can allow herself to have her body tended by others. Her hair is a focus around which she can enjoy gentle nurturance, motherly body care, long after she has left childhood behind.

Both of these reasons may apply just as much to men. Hairdressers tell us that modern men are showing as much concern about their hair as women. So, for both male and female movers, revisiting a trusted hairdresser can be a way of preserving identity, and being physically soothed through a disturbing transition.

Trips back to the community you are leaving will be important for many reasons. It will feel good to touch base with people who know you, value you, love you during the interlude before you feel known, valued, and loved by new people in a new place. Why not set a date for a reunion even before you leave (you can always change it later)?

But trips may have to be infrequent, for reasons of time or money. The next best thing can be planning your budget to include phone calls or E-mail, if you have a home computer.

"My phone bill was forty dollars for my first month here," said a single mover. "But still, that was less than a psychiatrist's fee!" Even when you can't have a two-way conversation, the voice of a loved one can be comforting. Why not ask special people to tape messages for you?

This may be a good moment to turn back to your Lifescan (Chapter 2), and identify things that have special meaning in your life and could be taken with you. Here are some ideas to get you started.

With your family, a close friend, or even alone, you might design your own rituals of continuity. For example, as you take a last swim at your favorite beach, why not gather some shells to take along? As you meander through the woodland you love, why not gather some pine cones and plan to hang them on the Christmas tree in your new home? As you have a last dinner at your favorite Greek restaurant, why not ask if you could buy a place mat or a mug?

Consider digging some favorite bulbs to plant in your new garden. Their first young shoots will signal that they are rooting themselves in your new home, and remind you that you are rooting too. Their blooms will help you stay connected with the place you left behind.

Food provides intense connections between past and present. What foods are important in your rituals and celebrations, or even your daily diet? If you are unlikely to find basmati rice or Hungarian paprika in your new town, lay in a supply to take along. Or arrange to order it from your favorite store.

For many movers, the first linkages between past and present are aroused by scent. Whether it's the scent of lilacs or Indian curry, that whiff stirs images of the past. Powerful emotions, too—a stab of sadness, a longing for what you've left. But the glad feelings infusing your memories will be rekindled too. They will flow into the present and permeate the new surround. They will strengthen the sense of positive connection.

As you start packing up, scan your possessions. Consider which ones are most strongly imbued with precious memories. Is it your son's discarded posters of the Grateful Dead? Is it your high school yearbook? Be cautious about consigning such things to the tag sale. Taking at least some of them along can reinforce your sense of continuity while you are in the midst of turbulent change.

As you pack, designate a particular box as your "security box." No, not for your insurance policies or your will, but for a selection of accessible things that will comfort you during the chaotic days or weeks after your arrival. It might be a loaf of sourdough pumpernickel, a musical tape or book—whatever you reach for when your world feels topsy-turvy.

Chapter 8 Exercises

EXERCISE A

Imagine that you have just received a phone call from a friend who said, "My sister lives in the same town you're moving to, and I told her that you'll be there soon. She offered to help you out, being sort of a sponsor, when you get there."

How might you respond to such an offer?

_____

_____

What would you like or expect your sponsor to do for you when you arrive in the new community?

_____

_____

Would you want to call her or have her call you?

_____

_____

Think about people you know who have recently moved. Ask these movers if, when, and how they found sponsors. Also, ask for suggestions for finding yourself a sponsor in your new community (e.g. schools, religious and/or professional organizations, neighborhood groups).

EXERCISE B

Rituals can help you carry memories of your old life into the new one, and can serve as important bridges into your new community.

List several of your daily rituals (e.g. jogging alone every morning, partners cooking dinner together every night, helping the kids with homework.

_____

_____

_____

_____

List several of your weekly rituals (e.g. excursions to the lake, shopping at the mall, attending religious services).

_____

_____

_____

_____

List several seasonal rituals (e.g. celebrating Thanksgiving with family or friends, going to the first football game, planting daffodil bulbs, attending the symphony series, hosting a Fourth of July picnic).

_____

_____

_____

_____

Look again at your lists of rituals. Which will be easy to continue in your new home and community? Which will be difficult to continue? Which rituals will you probably have to give up? What new rituals could you develop?

_____

_____

_____

_____

Try to find out about family and community rituals in your new area. Make believe you are taking an anthropology course, and your assignment is to learn about ten rituals in the community you will be living in. Gather information from regional or city newspapers and magazines, Chamber of Commerce, Newcomer's Club or Welcome Wagon, your realtor, your sponsor.

_____

_____

_____

_____

CHAPTER 9

Prepare Your Children: "How are We Going to Get this Whole House in a Truck?"

The time has come to help your children understand that the move is actually going to happen. Even if they've taken part in the decision to move, and in setting the date, it may not seem altogether real. Now we'll suggest ways to involve them constructively in the preparations.

🏠

MONITORING YOUR FEELINGS

Most communications about moving are laden with emotion. How you handle your own emotions sends important signals to them. If you try to be completely matter-of-fact, you may signal that it's not OK for them to express feelings—or even to have them. Yet a tidal wave of emotion from you could overwhelm them. Moderation is the name of the game.

So let's start with you. How are you feeling about this move—excited, relieved, ready to start packing? Or sad, angry, resentful? If you have a partner, how does s/he feel? You probably have mixed feelings; sorting them out helps you help your children.

Sharon, a lifelong Chicago resident, was devastated when her husband was offered a job in a small Texas town. "Art had been out of work for a couple of months, and our bills were piling up. We were desperate for him to get a job, and we thought anywhere would be okay if we were all together. So he applied for jobs all over. Then the offer came. I was stunned, but the alternative was no job and no money."

"That night I went into our daughter's room to tell her. Karen was nine, and she'd always been a rock-steady kind of kid—nothing ever seemed to upset her. I said, 'Honey, Daddy got a job today, but we have to move to Texas.' I just blurted it out. Well, Karen started to sob. She didn't talk, just sobbed. Then I burst into tears, and I was crying harder than she was. She stopped crying and looked at me like she didn't know what to do—I couldn't even talk. It probably scared her to death. What a great way to start off our move—with a mother who can't stop crying!"

Sharon did stop crying, of course, and helped her daughter deal with good-byes. But three years later, Sharon still recalls that anguished night. "I needed a few more days for my own grief and shock to come out. I was numb until I saw Karen cry, then all my grief came out onto her. So I spent the next few days, while Karen was in school, visiting or calling my close friends. I cried every time I told someone that we were leaving. My friends were wonderful, they hugged me, and a few cried right along with me. I remember wishing that I had cried first with my friends and then tried to tell Karen. I could have listened to her better that night."

What impact might your tears have on your children? They may worry that they did something wrong, and wonder if you'll still take care of them. It's important to reassure them, perhaps saying "I'm sad about saying good-bye to our house and all our friends. So I cry like you do when you're sad. I'm not upset with you. I love you, and after I stop crying I want you to tell me how you feel about this move."

But give yourself a chance to think and feel and talk about your move before you break the news to your children. Turn to your partner, a trusted friend, a colleague, or a clergy person.

If you're worried about telling your children, why do it alone? Ask someone to help you tell your child, but let that person know what specific kind of support you need. Do you want someone just to sit next to you, maybe holding your hand? Do you want that person to do the talking, or to take over if you start to cry?

OXYGEN FOR THE FAMILY

If you've traveled on airplanes, recall the emergency instructions: parents are advised to put their own oxygen masks on first, and then put masks on their children. That's a valuable metaphor. You'll take better care of your children during stressful times if you take good care of yourself. That means eating well, exercising, and getting enough rest. It means other things, too.

Try to involve your partner—if you have one—in the whole process of preparing for the move. That's traditionally been seen as women's work. Women have been expected, and have expected themselves, to do the sorting and packing, as well as the remembering and grieving, while male partners holed up in their offices and avoided the pain. But times have changed, and a couple who share the work, the pain, and the joy of moving set a fine example of teamwork for their children, and are better able to support their children through their transition.

Before you feel overwhelmed, send out an S.O.S. Ask for and accept help from friends, relatives, and neighbors. You'll need regular breaks from the packing and the children. But plan enjoyable times with your children every day too.

PREPARING CHILDREN OF ALL AGES

Ask other parents and children to tell you about their moves. You may get some good ideas about ways to handle tricky situations.

Let your children's teachers or caregivers know that you are in the throes of moving. Ask them to provide the extra attention and reassurance that children need during transitions.

Try to keep your children's routines for eating, sleeping, and playing as close to normal as possible. In the midst of all the changes occurring in your household, it is stabilizing for children to have some aspects of their lives stay the same.

If your child's reactions to moving worry you, talk them over with your health care provider. A physical problem may be contributing, or psychological help may be needed. And ask for health records before you leave (you will probably have to sign a Release Of Information form, and there may be a charge). For a child with a chronic illness like asthma or diabetes, they are essential in case emergency care is needed. For healthy children, immunization records will be needed by new schools and day-care centers. Gather a supply of medications, and include the prescriptions. And prepare a simple First Aid box for the transition.

PREPARING CHILDREN OF DIFFERENT AGES

Every child is unique, and reacts to new experiences in individual ways. But thoughts, feelings, and behavior are also shaped by the child's maturation. Now we'll look at how and why children of different ages are likely to respond to an upcoming move (review Chapter 3 also), and we'll suggest ways to involve them constructively in your preparations.

INFANTS (0-12 MONTHS)

"Our baby was only seven months old when we moved, and he didn't know what happened." Parents often say such things, and in a certain sense it's true. Infants don't understand concepts such as moving, home, or neighborhood. But even tiny babies react to what they see, hear, smell, touch, and taste. Some are surprisingly quick to protest changes.

Nancy moved with eleven-month-old twins. "Ed and Mike reacted differently," she recalls. "Mike didn't seem to pay attention. I had baskets of toys in every room. He'd sit and play, seeming oblivious to the packers and the mess. Ed watched me like a hawk, and followed me from room to room. If he couldn't see me, he'd start screaming and he noticed the changes. He'd crawl into a just-emptied room, and sit there looking around at the walls, as though he was stunned."

Mike seemed insulated from the commotion around him, but it was stressful for Ed, and he was too young to ask Nancy what was happening—why the household, with its familiar sounds, objects, textures, pathways for crawling, was changing.

It's not only the physical surroundings that change. Babies respond to a parent's change of mood and to tension within a family. They know when you sound different, when you hold them differently, and when you're slow in responding to their cries. If you're upset about the move, you baby will sense that. If you're distracted and busy with packing, your baby will notice that.

"Josh was six months old when we moved," remembers Trish. "I thought the move would be easy—he took two long naps every day and slept all night. When he was awake he played and cooed, and rolled around on the floor. Then I started packing, and his whole personality seemed to change! He cried all the time unless I carried him around. Luckily, my mother came to help. She took over the packing so I could play with Josh, or she'd take Josh for walks while I packed."

Your baby may react to the commotion by clinging and fussing more than usual, and being harder to console. Some resist bedtime, or waken during the night. So your baby may be more demanding just when you are busier than ever, leaving you frustrated and overwhelmed. This is the time for your S.O.S! But even that can go awry.

"Owen was nine months old when we moved," recalled Dena. "I couldn't do it alone—pack and watch him, too. So I hired a really nice woman to come help out. But If she tried to pick Owen up, he'd scream, and start reaching for me—he wouldn't have anything to do with her."

Owen was showing an anxiety about strangers that is typical for his age but, unfortunately, it converged with his anxiety about the changes at home. It might have been wise to introduce the baby-sitter sooner.

🏠

Here are specific suggestions to help prepare your baby for the move:

- Look again at OXYGEN FOR THE FAMILY.
- Keep your baby safe, especially if s/he is crawling or walking. You may be leaving doors open as you pack, and using toxic cleaning supplies, tools, and ladders. Babies

can find the deadliest household items in a matter of seconds.

- If you have an infant backpack or a stroller (with a safety belt), try using them as you work around your home. You can get your packing done, and the baby can watch and be with you, too. Or how about using a playpen with interesting toys while you're packing? Your baby will be able to see and hear you, and will be safe if you're out of the room.

- As you travel to your new home, will there be overnight stops? Some babies fuss when they're put to bed in unfamiliar places. You might introduce the portable crib (or whatever you'll be using) for naps or even a few nights before you leave.

TODDLERS (12-36 MONTHS)

"Nicholas started to walk three months ago, and he's been in constant motion ever since!" said Laura. "It's almost impossible to pack when he's around." Preparing to move with your toddler walking, climbing, and running all over is quite a challenge.

Your little one can't really understand what's going on. Even if s/he has an extensive vocabulary and your explanation is clear and careful, what does "moving" mean to a toddler? "Moving" is what a toy truck does when you push it, or what you do as you ride in a car. When you say, "We're going to be moving soon," your toddler probably thinks about being in motion.

The disruption of your household won't make sense, but s/he will be watching it closely. Toddlers quickly sense when you're busier and more distracted than usual. They may become fussier and demanding.

"I felt so frustrated by Paul when we moved," said Linda, his mother. "He was twenty-two months old. As soon as I started packing a box, he'd come over and grab my leg, or ask me to pick him up. I realized that he needed to be close to me so I kept a box of his favorite toys close by. I packed, and he sat next to my leg and played.

"I talked to him a lot—I'd tell him about the things I was putting in each box. Then he'd try to pack one of the toys from his basket. He was trying to help." Frustrated as she was, Linda understood and accommodated to Paul's heightened need for closeness and involvement.

"Frankie had only one tantrum as a two year old, and it was when we were moving," Carol, his mother, recalled. "I was packing some books and he came into the room. He began screaming and he couldn't seem to stop. Afterwards I realized how stressed we both were. I teach at night, so Frankie and I usually spend a lot of time together, especially in the mornings. Now I was waking up and packing, and not even having breakfast. The apartment was a mess, our TV had been packed, and I had become a one-woman moving company!" That tantrum alerted Carol that she and Frankie both needed help, and she found it from a friend.

Toddlers have strong emotions about what they observe but they can't yet use words to tell you how they feel. So they use their bodies—hitting, pushing, or biting—to express frustration, anger and confusion. Or they cry, cling to a parent, have a tantrum, revert to more babyish behavior—all typical ways of reacting to stress.

Here are more suggestions to help prepare your toddler for the move:
- Look again at OXYGEN FOR THE FAMILY
- Be on the alert for objects around the house that could harm your curious toddler. This is a time when even cautious parents accidentally leave doors open, and interesting-but-deadly household items are out in the open. Use safety gates to keep little ones out of danger

zones, such as bathrooms, kitchens, basements, and stairways.

- If your toddler seems interested, look together at some picture books about moving (we suggest some in our reading list).

- Most toddlers love to color, especially on large surfaces. As you pack, let your child decorate boxes for you. You'll be together, your toddler will be safe, and you'll get your work done.

- If your child enjoys listening to music, or cuddles with a blanket or stuffed animal at sleep time, be sure that these objects are set aside and not packed by mistake. Your toddler will be comforted by those "go-to-sleep" friends in transit and in your new home.

- Will your toddler sleep in a portable crib as you travel to your new home? It may ease the change if you introduce the crib for nap times or nighttimes before you leave.

- Look ahead: Whatever you're packing now, you'll soon be unpacking with your toddler around. On top of each box, place one or two small toys, books, or stuffed animals, then seal the box. In your new home, each box will have a surprise for your toddler to unpack and enjoy. Familiar objects are reassuring in a strange place.

PRESCHOOLERS (3-5)

By age three, language is usually developing well. Most preschoolers can grasp the notion of moving if it's put in simple, concrete terms.

"Our whole family is going to live in another place really soon. We'll bring our toys and clothes and furniture to our new home. We'll put our things in big boxes, and you'll be able to help."

Because preschoolers are developing a concept of time, they can understand when the move will take place if it's tied to their own experience. For example, "We'll move after the last day at nursery school." As the time draws closer, you might say, "You'll go to day care three more times, and sleep in our house four more times, and then we'll go." Keep explanations brief, and be prepared for a lot of questions. But there may be silence first as the child struggles with confusion.

"Ken didn't say a word when we told him about moving," remembered Nina. "He was three and a half. After we talked he went off to play with his trucks. I wondered if he understood what we had just said. After three or four days he suddenly asked 'How are we going to get this whole house into a truck?' I realized that he had been thinking about it all, but he needed me to explain step-by-step how we would move. Then he started asking questions. 'Can we take our cat? Can we take the dining room table?' I had to explain and reassure over and over again."

Once they begin to understand, how do preschoolers feel about moving? Parents describe a kaleidoscope of states—excitement, sadness, confusion, reluctance, anger, and acceptance—that may change from moment to moment.

"Kim has always talked well, so I kept asking her how she felt about leaving our house and her school friends," Alex, her father, recalled. "I had explained that she'd say good-bye to her teachers and friends, and we'd find a great new school for her in Boston. We talked a lot, but it was strange. One day she'd say, 'Can we move today?' or 'I want to go to my new house.' An hour later she'd say, 'I'm not moving' or 'I think we should live here forever.' "

Alex's first responses weren't helpful. "I'd say, 'Oh, you do so want to move—you just told me that!', or 'Moving is fun!'. She'd get mad at me and say, 'No. I'm not moving. It's a bad idea.' Then I realized that I should just listen, and even agree with her. She liked that—she probably felt I was finally taking her seriously. I'd say things like 'What do you think we should do?' The more I let her say that she didn't want to move, the more she eventually wanted to talk about our new house in Boston. Suddenly she became very interested in how we'd move and wanted to start packing her things. She was really helpful, once she decided to join in!"

Thoughts and feelings are expressed through behavior as well as words. Young children often enact moving in their play—cartons are fine make-believe houses, stuffed animals or dolls make fine movers. Playing out a life experience helps preschoolers feel more in charge of their lives, and observant parents or caregivers can learn how children imagine their moves by keeping an eye on their play.

Behavior is expressive in less desirable ways, too. Stressed preschoolers often act babyish, wanting to be dressed or fed, perhaps wetting the bed. They may be stubborn and show fierce tempers. These are signals that your preschooler needs extra reassurance.

Most preschoolers have close relationships with people outside the family. They are attached to special places too. So talk with your child about who and what s/he'll be leaving behind, and plan the good-byes.

"A week before we moved, I asked Max about saying good-bye," said Patty. "I told him that I'd miss June, our neighbor, and Glen, my boss. I asked him who he'd miss and he said, 'the river.' He meant it. We talked about where each of us loved to go, and we planned good-bye visits. We took one last walk to the river, and spent the afternoon throwing rocks in the water and walking on the shoreline. He came with me when I went to say good-bye to my favorite bakery. We did the places first, then we made good-bye visits to friends and neighbors."

Here are more suggestions to help prepare your preschooler.

- Look again at OXYGEN FOR THE FAMILY.
- Look back at COMMUNICATING WITH YOUR CHILD in Chapter 5.
- Include your preschooler in the sorting and packing. You might provide one large and one small moving box for each child. Tell them that they can pack special toys, books, stuffed animals, games, and other unbreakable treasures in each box. The large boxes can be loaded onto

the moving truck, while the smaller ones can be taken with you. You'll probably see a lot of packing, unpacking, and re-packing as your children make decisions about what to put in each box.

· Ask your preschooler to decorate the cartons as you pack. That's another way to help your child feel actively involved.
· Encourage your child to play "make believe" games about moving.
· Plan your good-byes to a few of your child's special friends and places (limit the number of farewells so your child won't feel overwhelmed). Help your child gather a few mementos—a seashell from the beach, a pine cone from the woods.
· Take photographs or videotapes of special people and places. Or encourage your child to include drawings and stories about them in the *Child's Book of Moving* (Exercise A).
· Help your children choose a few postcards, then self-address and stamp them. They can give cards to friends during good-bye visits, with a request to write soon. Each card that arrives in your new home will be a reminder that friends are thinking about them.
· Several days before departure, make a simple Moving Calendar together. Write in and draw a few things you'll do each day such as: Go to school, Eat breakfast with a friend, Go to the library. The last day on the calendar will include items such as: Moving truck comes today; Drive to our new home; Visit Grandma. Help your preschooler put the calendar where it can easily be seen.

ELEMENTARY SCHOOL AGE CHILDREN (6-10)

How do elementary school age children picture moving? Their images are drawn from memories, observations, fantasies, stories read and tales told by family and friends. They've overheard your conversations with other adults. They know about schoolmates or teachers who have moved in or out of their school. They have ideas gleaned from television, and they may have seen news pictures of the place you're moving to. It's a challenging task to help them separate the facts from the fantasies.

They will have a range of emotions about a move—sadness, anger, fear, as well as excitement, hope, and joy. Their emotions may be intense, but they may be hidden (remember eight-year-old Janice, in Chapter 3, who cried herself to sleep all summer before a move, but never told her parents about her sadness and fear). If children are ashamed of their feelings, or expect their parents will disapprove, a pillow may seem like the safest place to release them. But what a lonely place!

Most school-age children can talk about their ideas and feelings to friends and trusted adults. Ideas and feelings they're not aware of may be expressed in dreams. If your children describe dreams, you may get clues about their worries.

School children act out their attitudes about moving in their play. Being able to create their own scenarios helps them feel in charge of an experience that's largely out of their control. So try to keep an eye (and ear) on their play since it may reveal unspoken dreads. For example, in the make-believe move, the child and parents get separated and can't find each other again. Or the moving truck crashes and valued possessions get damaged. It helps to talk with the child about those scary ideas, and think of ways the fears can be eased..

Under stress, school children may revert to babyish behavior, become physically ill, or have outbursts of temper. They may become depressed, showing it in loss of interest in things they usually enjoy, trouble getting schoolwork done, unusual tiredness, sleeping and eating more or less than usual, looking gloomy, sounding hopeless.

Why might school age movers be so upset? Though their emotional bonds are still centered in their families, friendships are crucial too. Most children have best friends in whom they confide, and a clique or a gang as well. The support of those youngsters helps children ease out from the orbit of their families into a larger world. It helps them sort out their beliefs, values, and goals. It helps them establish their identities as special people—a good pitcher, a whiz at arithmetic, a loyal buddy.

Adults are important in those ways too—teachers, coaches, Scout Leaders, school bus drivers, librarians. Some of them are important as substitute mothers or fathers, especially for children with divorced or separated parents.

It's sad and scary to think about losing those special people. Children worry, "What if nobody likes me when I move, nobody wants to be my friend, nobody knows who I am? What if my best friend here forgets about me?" Best friends probably share the sadness.

"Ralph has known for a long time that we'd be leaving," said Ellen, who had shepherded him through four previous moves. "We promised him that we wouldn't move until he'd celebrated his eighth birthday. His party was last Sunday, and I noticed a peculiar numbness in him. Some of the kids told Ralph they'd really miss him, and asked if he could come back for their parties. He didn't answer and he's usually a talkative kid."

"On his last day in school, I stopped in to say good-bye to the teacher and see how Ralph was doing. A girl came up and said, 'Are you Ralph's mother? Please don't let him move—leave him here so he can be in our class!' Then a boy came up and hugged Ralph and said, 'I'm going to miss you.' But Ralph didn't show any kind of response."

"I realize he was overwhelmed by his friends' behavior—he wasn't prepared. We'd talked a lot about how each of us feels about moving, but we didn't talk about how our friends might feel and what they might say!"

Children have attachments to special places, too. These may be places where they developed important skills. They may worry about whether the new community will have a skating rink, a baseball field, a pond where favorite activities can continue. In Chapter 4, we've suggested gathering such information in advance. Now remind your children what you discovered.

Places may also be special because they are linked with meaningful relationships. Some may be unknown to parents—

secret parts of the neighborhood where children gather. But some are significant for both child and parent.

Ted lived in Idaho until he was ten, when he moved with his parents to Maine. Beforehand, his father, Paul, asked if there was anything special Ted would like to do to say good-bye. "Let's go sledding one more time on our sledding hill," Paul begged. "I want to say good-bye to the hill."

"I wanted to say good-bye to the hill, too," Paul recalled, "so I was excited when Ted asked if we could go. The next day we went sledding after school. Ted said he wanted to take one last ride. I started to feel very sad as I watched him get onto his sled. When he reached the bottom he yelled, 'One more time, Dad!' This went on for forty-five minutes—he kept taking one more ride." As the memory flooded him, Paul's eyes filled with tears. "He loved that hill and I had a lot of memories of my own, sledding with my kid. I took him there for the first time when he was a year old and we went every winter. I was going to miss the hill too, and I was scared we wouldn't find another one like it. When we got home that day, I promised him that the first thing we would do in Maine was go find another hill as big as our Idaho hill. We haven't found it yet."

We hope Paul and Ted will find that hill. It's risky to promise things you're not certain you can deliver.

Here are more suggestions to help prepare your school-age child.

- Some strategies for preschoolers will still be useful. Have another look. Your school-age child may think your *Child's Book of Moving* is too babyish, or s/he may enjoy it. Try it out.
- Ask your child how s/he would like to be involved in the planning.
- Include your child in discussions about the moving date, taking into account special events like birthdays, school plays, last game of the soccer season.

- If family members will move at separate times, reassure your child that the family isn't breaking up, and ask how s/he would like to stay in touch with the absent ones.
- As the moving date gets closer, make a calendar of events in the child's life, including such things as playtimes with friends, sports events, last day of school, day when the moving truck comes. This will help your child feel grounded amidst the confusion.
- Help your child plan good-bye visits, and write them on the calendar. Plan to go along if you're wanted. Remind your child that not only will s/he feel sad, but other people will, too.
- Take pictures of your home, neighborhood, school, special friends. Later, they can be gathered in a scrapbook.
- Make or buy an autograph book for your child to use for phone numbers, addresses, and messages from friends and teachers.
- If your budget allows, plan a good-bye party. Perhaps allow your child to choose the food, and to choose inexpensive gifts for friends.
- Use maps as you talk about going to your new home.
- As soon as you know you're moving, ask your children's teachers to prepare folders of their work, perhaps including math, writing, art work. Ask, too, for standardized test scores and descriptions of math, science and language arts curricula. Since teachers and administrators are busy, it's wisest to gather this information yourself before you leave. It will be helpful for your children's new teachers.
- If you know what school your child will attend, call or write to see if someone could send your child some school news or pictures. If you know what teacher your child will have, ask how new students are welcomed—some teachers ask pupils to write to incoming members of the class. Or help your child send for information about the new school and community. S/he will love receiving mail and having a personal collection of materials.
- If your child has special needs, contact the local chapter of the National Parent Network on Disabilities (see appendix).

- If you are committed to home teaching, contact the network of home-schooled children in the new community (see appendix).

Chapter 9 Exercises

EXERCISE A
YOUR CHILD'S BOOK OF MOVING

Writing and drawing in their own book is a splendid way for children to express ideas and feelings, portray fantasies, and ask indirect questions. It can help your children make sense of your move, and stay connected with their former home after you move. It can help you learn about what is important to them so you can help them through an unsettling but exciting transition.

1. OLDER TODDLERS AND PRESCHOOLERS

Most very young children love to draw. Offer them a sturdy set of crayons, magic markers, pencils, and huge sheets of paper. Ask your child to draw pictures of favorite toys, members of your family, special friends, pets, favorite teachers and/or caregivers. Suggest that your child draw a picture of him/herself in front of your home. It's best to keep your suggestions simple. We encourage you to get on the floor and give hands-on help. You can offer to label pictures: "This is a picture of a big moving truck that I saw today" or "This is me feeling sad when I say good-bye to my friends." When you have enough pictures, or your child is ready to do something else, staple all these pages together and make a cover: "Sarah's Big Book about Moving." Remember that young children have short attention spans, and some youngsters love to draw pictures–but not always about their family's move!

Another idea: Some children may prefer to buy a special notebook in which they can write and draw. Again, they'll need help from you in labeling pictures, and the drawings will probably be about more than just your family's move.

2. ELEMENTARY SCHOOL-AGE CHILDREN

Children in this age group are either very enthusiastic about writing and illustrating books, or are very reluctant to do so. Offer them the necessary materials—plenty of paper, good pencils, markers, crayons, and staplers—and express your interest in reading their books. Or help them buy notebooks or drawing pads. Some children may request that no one else read their books (that means YOU!).

Children who enjoy writing will need very little direction from you to get started. Others will welcome your ideas. Try the following unfinished sentences (we suggest one sentence per page). They can complete each one with words and pictures:

- My name is ___ and I am ___ years old. This is a picture of me:
- I like to play with ___. This is a picture of me playing with ___.
- I'm going to move soon to ___. This is a picture of me when I found out I'm moving:
- When you move, you have to say good-bye to a lot of people. Here is a picture of me saying good-bye to ___.
- We have a lot of things to move. Here is a picture of the things that I'm taking with me to our new home:
- My best friend is ___. We're friends because ___. Here is a picture of me with ___.
- This is a picture of me in my home. I live here with ___.
- The two things I like about where I live now are ___ and ___. Here is a picture of the things I like about living here.
- Two things I don't like about living here are ___ and ___. Here is a picture of the two things I don't like very much:
- My advice to other kids who have to move is always___ and never ___. Here is a picture about this:
- I wish my friends would___. Here is a picture about this.
- I wish my mom/dad wouldn't ___ . Here is a picture about this.
- The thing I like about moving is ___. Here is a picture about this.

- The thing I don't like about moving is ___. Here is a picture about this.
- Sometimes I wish ___. Here is a picture about this.

Add more ideas—yours and your child's. Consider making your own book with some of the same unfinished sentences, then read your responses to each other.

Children who prefer not to write their own book or keep a journal may enjoy making a scrapbook. Inexpensive photograph albums make excellent scrapbooks. Your child can save birthday party invitation, notes from friends, report cards, newspaper articles about their community, ticket stubs from sporting events, and many other mementos. For older children who find it difficult to write about emotions, making a scrapbook is a more comfortable way to express thoughts and feelings.

Encourage your children to keep their books, journals, and scrapbooks going throughout your family's move. They'll have much more to write about, draw, and collect as all of you move into your new home.

Here is a list of school and health items you might need right away in your new community. You may want to start collecting and organizing them as you prepare to move. We've also included a list of "comfort items" you might want to have on the trip to your new home.

Health-related items:

_____ Birth certificates
_____ Immunization records
_____ Health records
_____ Release of Information forms (ask your child's doctor about this)
_____ Prescriptions
_____ Medications
_____ First aid kit

School-related items:

_____ School records (transcripts, test scores, report cards etc.)
_____ Samples of your child's writing, artwork etc.
_____ Curriculum/program descriptions from the child's present school
_____ IEP (Individual Educational Plan) if your child is in a special education program (talk with your child's teachers and principal about this)

Comfort items:

_____ Stuffed animals
_____ Special toys
_____ Favorite blankets
_____ Books and music/story tapes
_____ Photographs of special people and places

CHAPTER 10

Getting Teens Ready: Easier Said than Done but Not Impossible

Adolescence is a time of rapid and bewildering change. There are hormonal shifts that spark aggressive and sexual urges. There is rapid physical growth and altered body contours. There are new ways of thinking, variable moods and emotions. Adolescents feel things with an intensity that is marvelous yet terrifying. They can go from a feeling of ecstatic togetherness to one of utter aloneness as a result of an unanswered phone call.

Adolescents continually strive to shape their personhood. They try on identities much as adults try on different dresses or neckties, expressing their shifting self-images through clothing that adults find bizarre, earrings that look strange, haircuts that are startling. Those adornments help them feel distinct from their parents and connected to their peers. Yet some of their clothing, whether it is a city boy's first tuxedo, or a rural teen's first blaze orange vest for hunting, helps them stay in touch with their family's heritage.

That heritage matters. Although adolescents strain at the yoke of parental control, their expressed wish for independence is not a wish for disconnection. Rather, it is a wish to have their individuality understood and accepted by the family. They rely on parents for boundaries that will keep them safe.

Adolescents test their strengths in feats of physical endurance, acts of bravery, and foolhardy risks. They show surprising resilience, yet they are profoundly vulnerable, too. The suicide rate is high, serious injuries from accidents are frequent, problems with substance abuse are common.

In the midst of so much inner turmoil, they need consistency and predictability around them. Unfortunately, a move strips those qualities away. In the midst of their faltering efforts to take charge of their lives, and to feel distinct from their parents, close friends keep them grounded, rooted, safe. Sadly, a move disrupts those needed friendships. Teenagers who move describe major realms of loss (see Chapter 3). Loss of identity and loss of friends are the most disturbing.

DEALING WITH PAIN

Adolescents do survive their moves and may later recognize some positive benefits. But their memories are often filled with pain.

It may be hard for you to let yourself be aware of your teenager's distress about moving. It is difficult for most parents to do things that hurt their offspring. Deciding on a move that will disrupt your teen's life will probably make you feel regretful, even guilty. Guilty parents can hardly bear to listen to their youngsters' sadness and anger.

Too, you may be in turmoil yourself, and being faced with your teen's troubled feelings seems like an overload. Or you may be delighted about moving, and find it hard to imagine that they feel different. For any of these reasons, you're tempted to deny their pain and urge them to focus only on the positive aspects of moving. Yet that leaves the adolescent feeling alone, unheard, and anxious.

It's more constructive for parents to accept the responsibility for having made a distressing choice, and then try to listen, understand, and validate the teen's feelings. If you feel overwhelmed and your teenager's storms are unbearable, it is best to be frank: "I'm upset about this move myself, and right now I can't listen to you the way I'd like." Encourage your youngsters to turn to other supportive people (while you do the same), promising that you'll listen to their reactions as soon as you can.

Point out that you'll be working together to make the most positive transition possible. That will include finding the best ways to say good-bye, to preserve meaningful connections and to build bridges into the new life. In this move in which they lose much control over their lives, it's important to allow teens some choices about how to go through it.

But be clear about what decisions they can influence and which they cannot. It would be unfair to give the impression that they can affect decisions that have already been made, or that they can make choices that are unrealistic for the family.

Your way and your youngsters' ways of preparing for a move may be different. At the end of this chapter, there is a section just for teens. If you read it, try not to check up on whether your teens have followed our suggestions. Your checking may spur them to refuse, especially if they're angry about the move. Too, they need to find their own balance between privacy and sharing their thoughts and feelings with you.

SAYING GOOD-BYE

One of fifteen-year-old Chuck's big regrets was that he didn't say good-bye to his friends before he and his family moved to Virginia. "It hit me halfway down the New Jersey Turnpike. I'm like, I didn't say good-bye to the guys. I kept thinking I'd do it just before we left, then suddenly it was pack-up day, then we were heading south in the car with the U-Haul behind us, and it was too late."

Few people like good-byes. They can be particularly hard for teens, who say good-bye to many things as they grow up. You can't make good-byes happen, but you can set an example and provide opportunities.

You could offer to have a farewell party for your teens' friends, and help them plan it and prepare the food and drink. They may not want one, though, fearing the intense emotions that might get loose. Gatherings may be easier if they are not labeled as farewell parties. Instead, propose "One last party for the team, for the band, or for your friends."

If a party doesn't appeal, you might suggest that they take their best friends out for pizza, and help with the cost. Or you might take over their paper route so they can go camping overnight with their closest friend. One mother allowed her son and his best buddy to skip school to attend a last Red Sox game together. Whatever you and your teens decide, your offers will convey your understanding that leaving special people is a significant, sad experience.

STAYING CONNECTED

Good-byes don't have to be for forever. Brainstorm with your teens, planning ways they can stay connected. If you can afford it, they might plan to visit their old friends during summer or Christmas vacations.

Some teens (not many) still write letters. Or you might buy them an inexpensive cassette recorder and mailers for audio tapes that will carry messages back and forth. If you and their friends have video recorders, they can exchange videos. More and more teens use E-mail to stay in touch.

The most comfortable way for teens to connect is probably by phone. While frequent long-distance calls add up to a large bill, voice contact with old friends is very helpful in the early stages after a move. Try working out an arrangement like this: your teens will be allowed two hours of phone calls per week for two weeks, then one hour per week for two weeks, then one hour per month. There are times (e.g. late at night when many teens like to talk on the phone anyway) when inexpensive phone rates go into effect. Teens can also help pay for the calls. An hour at night may cost eight dollars, not much more than a movie or a pizza.

BUILDING BRIDGES

Although they face similar challenges in their development, each teenager is unique. Through a combination of inborn temperament and life experience, they may be calm or excitable, adaptable or rigid. They may be outgoing and gregarious, or shy and withdrawn. They differ in their talents, and in what helps them feel good about themselves.

If there is one principle to remember in helping teens prepare for a move, it is PLAY TO THEIR STRENGTHS. Consider what they do well and what they love, and plan ways to maximize opportunities for those activities after the move. For example, a family whose daughter was an avid musician arranged for her to attend a music camp the summer before she moved to a new school. They knew that band members from that school attended the camp. When the girl started school, she already knew some students, and she was accepted by the group whose activities centered around the band.

"I needed to have something to look forward to," said Robbie, a sixteen-year-old who had strenuously resisted his family's cross-country move. "The only thing that kept me going was a letter I got from the baseball coach saying he was looking forward to having me on the team. I carried it around with me the whole month before we moved, and when I got too discouraged, I'd sneak off somewhere and read it."

EXPLORING SCHOOLS

The baseball coach knew about Robbie because Robbie's family had investigated high schools before moving. This is very important in preparing for your teenager's move. The choice of high school (if there's more than one) will influence where you will want to live in the new community. Also, schools can have a large influence on how adolescents cope with stress.

If possible, visit with your teen. Many important characteristics of a school were discussed in Chapter 9. But some questions are especially important for an adolescent.

How structured is the school? For example, are students expected to stay on the grounds even when they don't have classes? Is there a policy about smoking, about drug usage, about sexual activity (yes, it may happen in the parking lot)? How are infractions of school rules handled? How are special conditions such as pregnancy dealt with?

How safe is the school? Have there been incidents of violence, with or without deadly weapons? How have they been handled?

What are the educational goals? For example, what proportion of students are in a vocational/trade school track? Can they earn vocational credits? What proportion are bound for two-year college, for four-year college? Are there extra classes to prepare for SATs? How is it decided which track each student will be placed in? What special educational services are provided in the district?

Keeping in mind your youngsters' interests and talents, find out if the school provides the needed facilities and programs. Find out if there are people in the school—such as Robbie's baseball coach—that your youngsters can connect with even before the move. Inquire how newcomers are gathered into the fold. Keep in mind that it may be best for your teen to move at a different time from you (see Chapter 6), and ask how school staff would react to that.

How might you gather this information? The principal or school counselor, or both, can be very helpful, especially if you have set up an appointment in advance. If your youngster has special needs—a learning disability or a chronic health problem, it can be useful to have a conference with the head of the special education department and/or the school nurse. Ask about support groups for parents of children with special needs, as well as groups for the youngsters. Ask also for the names and phone numbers of the head of the P.T.O., and the class parent of the grade your teen will enter.

You may be unable to make an advance visit. Arranging for a phone conference with a member of the counseling department is the next best bridge. Ask about paperwork to be done now. It is likely to include: information forms about your teenager, medical emergency instructions, record release forms so the new school can get information from the present school, and a federally mandated English as a Second Language Questionnaire. Ask for a course description catalogue, so your teen can begin thinking about what courses to take. Then set up an appointment to meet with a staff member soon after your arrival, and arrange an orientation for your teenager.

Finally, look over the exercises in Chapter 9. We include a checklist of the educational and health records you will need for your move.

EXPLORING NEIGHBORHOODS

We've discussed neighborhoods in Chapters 4 and 9. Why not review those now? Remember that a neighborhood that looks "nice" to adult eyes may not seem nice in the eyes of a teen. For example, a move into an urban apartment close to concert halls and museums may seem wonderful to you. But if your daughter is a cross-country runner, it could seem like the eighth circle of Dante's Inferno!

Steve, a seventeen-year-old who was treated for alcohol and drug abuse, dated his addiction to a time shortly after his father's promotion. His family moved from a "blue collar" city neighborhood where Steve would happily "hang out and shoot hoops" with his friends to an upper middle class suburban neighborhood where he felt totally out of place. The only teens Steve was comfortable with there were in a small group of alienated pot smokers. They, like he, felt marginal.

MOVING AND COLLEGE STUDENTS

It is easy to assume that your move only affects offspring who are still at home. But if you have lived in a home for a long time, it has powerful meanings for all the youngsters who grew up there. For them, as for you, it has probably been a safe, reliable refuge. It has been a place where they had the sense of belonging, a place where their abilities and ideas, as well as their emotions, could be expressed and appreciated. It has been a place where relationships developed and important experiences occurred—a place filled with significant memories. Even coupled adults in their fifties talk about how sad they felt when their aging parents decided to sell the family home and move into a small apartment.

For adolescents and young adults who are away in college or professional school, the place they grew up in is still their psychological home, even if they only live there for a few days at holiday time. They use various strategies to preserve their space at home. They leave pets for their parents to care for, boxes of prom dresses, or old baseball mitts in the attic. Their images of home can be comforting and reassuring as they move out into the world on their own.

Leaving their home is not the same as losing it. When you move, they lose it. They need to be involved in giving it up. For example, you will have to make choices about what gets moved, what gets left behind, and what gets consigned to the yard sale or dump. Your absent offspring should have a major say about their own possessions, and some say about possessions that are part of the family history. Those choices arouse strong emotions that need to be expressed.

If you are moving far away, your college-age youngsters will have to decide whether to spend vacations in their home town, away from you but among their high school friends, or with you and away from those old friends. It's wise to talk that over before you move.

Sandy's solution, when her family moved from Iowa to New Hampshire while she was in college, was to visit her new home over Christmas vacation, and to visit relatives and friends in Iowa during Spring Break. When she came north for Christmas, she would bring one or two college friends with her. In that way, she could go skiing or out for a beer with friends even though she knew nobody her age in the new town. You and your offspring will think of other strategies along those lines.

BEING AVAILABLE

Your most important goal in helping your adolescents prepare for the move should be to stay available to them as a reliable source of understanding and support—someone who gives them freedom to make small mistakes and tries to prevent them from making big ones, and someone they can still turn to when it feels that things just aren't working and nobody cares. Amidst your own turmoil, that may be easier said than done. This is the time to draw on all the help you can find.

A LETTER TO A TEENAGER FACED WITH MOVING

Dear Teenage Mover,

This is to wish you good luck on your move and to make some suggestions. They are based on things other teens found helpful. Pick those you can use and don't worry about the others.

Don't try to deal with your feelings about the move alone. Moving is upsetting and you need at least one person you can talk to. If you can turn to one or both parents, that's great, but moving isn't easy for them either. They may have less time or energy available to help you than they have in the past. If you'd like their help, it's fair to ask for what you need, but try to be understanding if they can't provide it.

Grandparents, uncles or aunts can be helpful too. Or friends, guidance counselors, coaches, teachers, ministers or bosses. Whoever it may be, it's important to have someone. Figure out a way to stay in touch with this helpful person, since you'll have some hard times after the move too.

Even though good-byes are hard, it's important to say good-bye to friends and plan how to stay in touch after you go.

Consider keeping a freewriting journal. Freewriting is done by writing for fifteen minutes as fast as you can, not stopping to consider punctuation, spelling, grammar, or how you think a teacher or anyone else would judge your writing. Don't worry if you repeat yourself. During the fifteen minutes don't stop. If you don't know what to say next, write down "I don't know what to say" until something comes along. Write down what seems to you to be true about the world outside you or the feelings inside you. Don't make excuses; keep writing as fast as you can.

Your freewriting is yours and you should keep it somewhere private. You may want to share it with your parents or someone else, but it's important that you do it for yourself, not for others.

You're probably angry and sad about having to move. Those are normal feelings. But if you're so sad or angry that you've thought about hurting yourself, getting help is urgent. Tell your parents. Talk to a school guidance counselor, your doctor, a community hotline or your community mental health service. Sadness sometimes shows up as lack of energy, trouble sleeping, or loss of appetite. These states, too, are reasons for getting professional help.

Although it's normal to worry about life after the move ("Will I make any friends?" "Will I make the track team?" "Will I get into the honors English class?"), try not to let that "parade of imaginary horribles" interfere with what you should be doing now. If they do, talk them over with the person you trust.

Focusing on your goals—for the next year, the next three years, the next five years—may help you plan for the move and deal with the pain.

Try to connect with someone in your new school. We've enclosed a sample letter you could send to a coach, a band director, etc. It's hard to send letters to people you don't know. You may decide that it's something you don't want to do, or you may want to write a letter in your own way.

Are there other ways you could make a connection in your new town? Have you worked at McDonalds? Is there a McDonalds in your new town? If so, get your supervisor to write a letter of recommendation for you. Were you active in your church youth group? Is there a similar group in the town you are moving to? Have you worked as a volunteer in the hospital, or a nursing home? Do you like to go mountain biking? Is there a bike shop in your new town? If so, write them and see if they can give you the names of some other mountain bikers. Why not review your Lifescan to search for other ideas?

Many people use drugs, alcohol, or cigarettes to cope with bad moods, or sad and lonely feelings. What's more, drinking or smoking with other people can seem like an easy way to make new friends. But watch out. Those quick solutions lead to worse problems down the road.

Most of the teenagers we talked to said moving was a hard, upsetting experience. But almost all of them also said you should be hopeful. They made new friends, found new places they liked, and adjusted to the move. Some of them have since gone back to their old towns for college or jobs. Others have settled happily in their new towns.

We hope our suggestions will help you prepare for the changes down the road. If there are things we left out that could help other teenagers faced with moving, please write us so we can include them in future editions of this book.

With our good wishes,

Audrey McCollum
Nadia Jensen
Stuart Copans

A SAMPLE LETTER TO A COACH

117 Stage Road
Brattleboro, Vermont 05301
April 1, 1994

Mr. Wiley Coyote
Coach, Track Team
South Tucson High School
17 Old Tucson Road
Tucson, Arizona 09776

Dear Mr. Coyote,

I am writing because I will be moving from Brattleboro, Vermont, to Tucson next August, and will be a tenth grade student at South Tucson High School. I have been on the track team at my present high school, and have run in the 800 and 1500 meter races, and the 4-400 relay. My best times have been 2:11 in the 800 and 4:27 in the 1500.

I would be interested in running on the track team in Tucson, and would appreciate it if you could write me about the team, and could tell me if any members of the team will be working out this summer, so I could begin running with them in August.

With thanks for your help,
Sincerely yours,
Polly or Peter Roadrunner

SECTION THREE

Building Your New Lives

CHAPTER 11

Limbo: When Will this Ever Feel Like Home

AN EXCERPT FROM SYLVIA'S JOURNAL

December 30th. At 2:30 a.m., we arrived at our new house in the North. Our daughter greeted us with a woeful tale. There was a storm, she said, and the power went out, and there was no heat, so the pipes froze and one of them burst, and water flooded the first floor, and most of that froze too.

So we huddled on the dry floor upstairs, taking our golden retriever between us for warmth. We dozed until the cold penetrated so deeply that it was unbearable to lie still.

Dawn came and men came soon after—electricians, plumbers, and movers carrying furniture and huge cartons to put where? where? We stumbled around, unwashed, unshaven, uncombed, and then after hours and hours the door opened one last time and there stood my husband's new chief with a smile of greeting and a casserole. Meat and potatoes. Warm, cozy mashed potatoes.

"Welcome to Northland," he said.

YOUR OWN UPHEAVAL

It's unlikely that your arrival in your new home will be a soap opera, as Sylvia's was. But there will probably be chaos—around you and inside of you too.

"I'm afraid I'm going to lose it!" Andrea, a recent mover, told an old friend over the phone.

"What does that mean—are you going to murder the kids, run over your husband, or run screaming out of your house until you disappear over the horizon, leaving behind little clouds of dust like a cartoon character?" asked Jeff, thinking a little humor might ease the tension.

"All of the above," said Andrea, sounding as though she meant it.

Even if you are delighted to be moving, there are good reasons why you, too, may reach the brink of "losing it."

First of all, whether your previous home was a tiny apartment or a mansion, whether or not you liked the location or the layout, it probably felt like a haven. It was a place where you belonged, where your tastes, values, and abilities could be expressed and appreciated by others. It was a place where relationships developed and important experiences occurred. And it was a familiar place—you knew your way around and how to make things work.

Your previous home had important meanings, and the place that will become your home has none of those yet. You are in limbo. Although you don't share the tragic plight of those who are physically homeless, psychological homelessness can feel bleak.

Yes, it can be exhilarating to start putting your imprint on your new place. But to do that effectively, you need to organize the accouterments of daily living. No matter how carefully you've planned the packing, things will be misplaced and go awry.

"It's very confusing not knowing where things are. Old people get confused," said seventy-nine-year-old Jennifer, who moved from her cherished family home to smaller quarters. "And it makes me feel anxious. I feel anxious about everything. Tell your readers not to wait until they're old to make their moves." But young movers feel unsettled, too.

"It's exasperating because you can't find things," said twenty-two-year-old Mona. "You want to write, and the pencil has a broken point, and you can't find the pencil sharpener, and you don't want to buy a new one because you know it's there somewhere." The same thing can happen with the can opener, the toaster oven, the hangers for your clothes.

People need some sense of mastery over their surroundings. Right now, it seems as though you've lost control. Your sense of safety in a familiar, predictable haven has been suspended. Your sense of competence has been peeled away—and competence is a foundation of self-esteem.

Jennifer felt bathed in anxiety, Andrea felt at the brink of "losing it." Both women were saying they were overwhelmed. Yet Mona's exasperation was less intense and she took it in stride. Movers respond to chaos in individual ways, influenced by their age, their life experience, their personalities, their health, the circumstances of moving, and their current relationships.

Their bodies may express their emotional pain through headaches, back aches, stomach aches. A chronic illness like asthma or rheumatoid arthritis may take a turn for the worse. They may lose interest in food or start snacking non-stop. They may toss and turn instead of sleeping at night, and feel deeply tired all day.

They may feel confused, have trouble concentrating, and thoughts may be racing through their minds. Their memories may seem as full of holes as a Swiss cheese.

Their moods may see-saw up and down, with storms of irritability or crying. They may feel edgy, easily frustrated, more sensitive to hurts than usual, or too ready to pick a fight. They may have nightmares, or feel an unusual amount of fear and dread. Women susceptible to premenstrual syndrome, PMS, may find that their typical mood swings are more intense.

All of these states are common responses to the upheaval of moving. However, they are also signaling that an unhealthy level of stress is building up inside the mover.

So what about you? What warning signs are you noticing in yourself? What strategies might you use to avoid becoming physically or psychologically overwhelmed? We'll give you our ideas, but, first, look back at Exercise A5 and A6 at the end of Chapter 3. Or, if you're not using the exercises, think back to other stressful transitions in your life. Who helped you get through them? How did those people help? How did you take care of yourself? Can you use similar strategies now?

HELPFUL STRATEGIES

INVOLVING OTHERS

In many traditional families, it was expected that the work of moving would be carried out by the woman, and the expectation has lingered. But it's a high-risk expectation. The woman can readily be overwhelmed and, because of that, have little energy available for herself, her partner, or her children. She will suffer, family relationships will suffer, and the family will miss out on the satisfying experience of taking on a challenge together.

If you have a partner or children, it's important to involve them as soon as possible in negotiating who will be responsible for what. Think and talk about what each of you enjoys doing and what each of you hates doing, and divide up the tasks according to those preferences (as well as the ages of your children, of course).

Both adult partners should commit themselves to taking time off from their employment during the period of upheaval. Since most new jobs or educational programs have specific starting dates, that will mean setting your moving date to allow for a cushion of time in which some of the chaos can be absorbed. Or it will mean negotiating time off from your new job so that you can work with your partner at home. If you have children, that gives them a fine example of job sharing.

If you're moving as a single person, or if your partner is truly unavailable, send out an S.O.S. to relatives and friends from out of town, or neighbors and colleagues in your new community. Firm up your ideas about what you need—someone to go jogging with you, someone to locate a good plumber, someone to pull the tape off the packing boxes and (maybe more important) to keep you company in the midst of the chaos.

Hopefully, whether you're single or coupled, you will have tried to line up a sponsor in advance of moving (see Chapter 8). If you haven't succeeded, do keep trying. As you meet new people, let it be known that you're looking for someone to show you the ropes—someone to help you understand the community, someone to help you locate the goods and services you'll need during your transition.

When Ellen and Ron made their fifth move, their realtor had slipped an announcement of their impending arrival into the mailboxes of neighbors along the street. Within days, neighbors began coming to welcome them. If you have a realtor, it's something you might ask her to do for you.

Reaching out to new people is traditional in some regions of the country, and in certain neighborhoods, but not in others. You'll know what to expect if you have asked in advance. If not, try to find out now from your sponsor, neighbors, or colleagues. If nobody stops in or phones you, you'll understand that the local people are wary of strangers, or unaccustomed to rituals of welcome. Hopefully, you won't take it as a personal rejection.

You'll need to persist in finding the help you need. The nearest convenience store, the branch post office, the local library, your church, the Newcomers' Club are more good places to start asking.

ESTABLISHING PRIORITIES

As soon as possible, decide which realms of your home-to-be need to be reconstructed first. What aspect of your daily life feels most crucial to your well-being? What space and equipment will that require? Do you most need a functioning center for cooking and eating? Do you need the private refuge of your bedroom, with your favorite books at hand? Do you need your smartest clothes hanging and ready to go?

If you have a partner and/or children, ask them what they need first to feel safe and comfortable. Responding to their needs will help your own peace of mind—especially if it means that the children sleep through the night! But let the family know what you need, too. Then, *together,* establish a rough timetable for the tasks to be tackled.

SETTING YOUR PACE

Some movers find confusion so unbearable that they unpack non-stop until everything is in place. If disorder and loss of control make you anxious, your needs should be respected. But try, try, try to let yourself ask for help as you carry out your blitz.

Even if you can tolerate some chaos, you're probably eager for your new place to look, feel, smell, and sound just the way you want it. But it may take many weeks or months before the colors of the walls, the patterns of the fabrics, the arrangement of the furniture, the hanging of paintings, or the placement of mementos feel just right.

Many movers have to accept rented quarters even if they hope ultimately to buy. If it's a furnished place, the owner's taste may clash with your own. If it's unfurnished, there are probably restrictions in the lease—maybe you won't be allowed to attach your shelves to the wall.

Whether you rent or buy, you may not have the funds to decorate the way you'd like. You may have to tolerate frustration and disappointment as you set some dreams aside and work out compromises. Your energy will probably flag, and the days won't have enough hours to get everything accomplished.

For all of those reasons, the feeling of being at home is rarely recaptured quickly. So why undertake an exercise in futility? Why push yourself to the point of exhaustion, trying to avoid the limbo of homelessness rather than allowing yourself to ride through it? Throw some bright cloths over the unpacked boxes, tape your favorite poster onto the refrigerator, and go out to have some fun.

REPLENISHING YOURSELVES

Adults as well as children need some equivalent of the security blanket that Charles Schulz' winsome Linus clutches to help him face the world. Hopefully, you packed a security box for yourself, containing a few things that help you feel safe and content—your favorite tape or CD, your special blend of coffee, the Frisbee you use to play with your dog.

But those things will only comfort you if you use them! It's essential to take breaks during the days, weeks, or even months while you're unpacking and sorting and arranging—an interlude while you're still in limbo.

Sylvia and her family turned their backs on the frozen shambles in their new house, and celebrated the first day of their new life by skiing (the dog didn't get to go, and expressed herself by adding another puddle to the carpet). Physical activity is a splendid way to release tension—in fact, it can alter chemicals in the brain and brighten moods. Could you take a long, rhythmical walk, bike ride, or swim? Could you let go of your frustration by smashing a tennis ball or hurling a snow ball?

If you've never been an athletic person, you probably won't feel like starting now. But have you considered yoga or meditation? There may be classes in the new community that you could join right now. If not, the library or bookstore probably has books or videos that can help you learn some simple techniques quickly.

There are other ways of replenishing yourself through a brief Time-out. Why not take a nap? Ensuring that you're getting enough sleep is essential during stressful times. If a nap leaves you groggy and grouchy, try a Time-out for listening to music or reading. Enjoy your favorite radio program, or tune in on a familiar drama on TV. Those remembered voices can be consoling, and help you feel less alone.

Think of foods that comfort you, as well as keeping your energy level high. The mashed potato casserole brought to Sylvia and her family warmed them deeply—emotionally as well as physically. Hot soups, good breads—there are many foods that are both healthful and reassuring.

Humor can be healing—in fact, it's been found to speed recovery from illness. Some people can blow off a huge amount of tension in a fit of giggles. Help the process along by searching out the funniest story in the newspapers, or the most absurd cartoon, or by renting a video comedy.

Use a Time-out to go exploring, hunting down one of the places that matters most to you or your family—the nearest lake, the ice cream shop. You'll familiarize yourself with your new environs and boost your self-confidence.

"Sometimes I have a terrifying image of endless supermarket aisles," a frequent mover admitted. "I think of the numerous supermarkets I've had to find my way through, finding how and where the food is arranged, over and over again. It seems like a metaphor for having to discover and master a new environment over and over again." This was a woman who expected herself to do the central work of moving for her family. Had she felt justified in involving them directly, the dreaded trips to new supermarkets might have become a shared adventure.

If you're a single mover and wary of exploring strange places on your own, this is another time to call on your sponsor, a neighbor, relative, or colleague for a brief outing together.

There are many ways to replenish yourself. You may already know what works best. If you don't, this is the time to find out by trying different strategies, and by letting your loved ones know how you're feeling, how you'd like to be feeling, and what you think might help.

If you're not paying attention to your own well-being, that's a danger sign. It may signal that you're sliding into a state of psychological depression, and you may need professional help. We'll say more about that in Chapter 13.

FOSTERING RECONNECTION

Movers can experience powerful feelings of psychological reconnection when a sight, sound, touch, or smell stirs forgotten images of the past. Sometimes it happens by chance. Reni came out of a shop one day, thirteen months after her move, and noticed the aroma of Mediterranean food—a tantalizing melange of garlic, oregano, tomato—and her thoughts flew back to Italy, where she had happily lived. "That whiff made the sky seem brighter and the grass seem greener." A gladness crept under the cloak of depression that had shrouded Reni since her move.

One rainy day in April, four months after Sylvia's move, her husband phoned. "Come into town if you can, and walk past the white church. There's something I want you to see." Sylvia did, and she wrote in her journal, *The rain was gentle, coaxing up the earth smell from the newly thawed ground. And next to the church there was a sweep of cobalt blue, hundreds of Siberian Scillas freshly washed and teased into a dance by the falling raindrops. I remembered an English woodland where, twenty-five years ago, I walked in the early spring with my husband and infant daughter. The ground was carpeted with bluebells as far as we could see. The joy of that day welled up and infused this moment.*

You can foster such experiences, coaxing glad feelings from the past to flow into the present and permeate your new surroundings. Some of the things in your "security box" are intended to do that, but go further. Plant the cuttings or the flower bulbs you brought from your previous home, search out the pizza parlor with the nostalgic aroma. Look back at the Special Places you listed in your Lifescan, and see if you can find their counterparts here.

Feeling at home encompasses many things. Although most people need a room, apartment, or house that is a physical and psychological haven, feeling at home usually includes a sense of positive connection to a human community outside the dwelling. Reclaiming your identity, which we'll consider in the next chapter, is crucial in developing that.

Chapter 11 Exercises

You will probably feel in a state of limbo after you move. We've given examples of things that can help. Now draw on your own experience.

EXERCISE A

FIRST: Think about things you've done in previous homes and communities to feel more settled. List your ideas below.

_____

_____

_____

_____

_____

_____

NEXT: Talk over your ideas with your partner and/or close friends. Ask what they've done to help themselves feel at home after a move. List the ideas you've collected below. Maybe you can create some new "moving in" traditions in your new home and workplace.

_____

_____

_____

_____

_____

_____

FINALLY: As you try out some of these strategies, keep in mind that feeling at home develops slowly, and sometimes in unexpected ways.

EXERCISE B

- Begin to keep a journal about your move. Each evening, spend a few minutes writing about some of the people you met that day, what you learned about these people, and what you learned about your new community. During this interlude, while you're deluged with new information, experiences, and impressions, a journal will help you keep them sorted out and anchored in your mind.

- In the same journal, keep a daily record of your mood, your energy level, any physical symptoms, and any special events that happened that day. That record can help in several ways.

- First, if you have a really blue day, it can be reassuring to read that you felt optimistic and energetic three days before.

- Second, you may notice that certain kinds of happenings either lift or dampen your mood—that can clue you in to what you need to seek out or avoid.

- Third, if you notice that your mood is getting steadily blacker, or that you're having a lot of physical symptoms, you may realize that you need to send out an S.O.S.

CHAPTER 12

Reclaiming Your Identity: Who are You Anyway?

"I feel invisible." "It's as though nobody sees me." "Nobody seems to know who I really am." Such feelings are among the most powerful psychological threats that movers can face. The eerie state of seeming not to exist in other people's consciousness reflects the mover's loss of identity (see Chapter 3). Reclaiming some strands of identity is a central challenge after your move.

MOVERS WITH "BUILT-IN" IDENTITIES

Although people have many identities, their occupational identity is probably in the forefront during a move. A person who moves to become a student or to take a new job has a visible, ready-made identity that serves as a bridge through the transition. It may be a sturdy bridge or a rickety one.

Ben, for example, who followed a career trajectory as an engineer, found relocation to be "as easy as getting off one train and onto another." Through his several moves, his identity as an engineer remained intact. Scott's experience was far less smooth. If Ben recalled only the sunny side, Scott remembered that there was a shadow side too.

"How was it really for you?" asked Sylvia as she and Scott reminisced several years after their tumultuous move.

"It was a lot of things," said Scott, who had accepted a complex leadership position. "I didn't find what I'd been told I'd find, so it was like walking down unfamiliar pathways. I felt pretty unsure of myself."

"But you had an instant identity. Didn't that help?" asked Sylvia.

"Sure it helped," said Scott, "but people had different attitudes about it so it wasn't always the plus you thought it was."

When Scott walked through his office door, he walked into a web of expectations that his co-workers had formed before he arrived. Some hoped he would be a clone of his predecessor, some hoped he would be radically different. They expected that he would accomplish certain things, and that, through his efforts, certain things would be provided for them and for his firm. Some of the expectations were realistic, some were fanciful.

For Scott, the expectations were both stimulating and burdensome. He worried about whether he'd be able to measure up. Would he fail the people who wanted so much from him? Would he fail himself by being unable to use his skills effectively? Would he fail his wife by pulling her through a major upheaval without a positive outcome?

"I felt lonely too," Scott went on. "There wasn't anybody as a sort of mentor or person I could confide in."

"But you had a whole support structure in place, didn't you—your own staff as well as colleagues?" Sylvia said in surprise.

"Well, maybe I did in a certain sense," Scott said. "But some people resented the changes I wanted to make, and others were just plain competitive. I didn't know who was an ally and who wasn't." There were attitudes and emotions ready to be attached to Scott just because of his identity as a leader. There were envy, resentment and rivalrous feelings as well as respect and optimism.

We suspect that Scott's memories of his experience were more realistic than Ben's. Clearly, a "built-in identity" is not a panacea— it can be the source of many tensions. Yet, since it protects the mover against feeling invisible, it can be sustaining too.

MOVERS WITH AN UNCERTAIN IDENTITY

"When I was offered this fellowship in environmental studies, I accepted because I thought my husband could pursue his own research here too," recalled Gladys. "Arthur was retired, so he could work anywhere. I thought the library and the community of scholars here would be attractive to him. But after I'd accepted, he got cold feet and decided not to come. He thought it would make him seem unmanly to be following his wife." Gladys would have a highly visible identity. Arthur would have worked in the shadows.

Sad tales like Gladys' are less common now. Some "following" partners are men. Committed to supporting their wives' careers, some are willing to risk not finding work in their own chosen fields. Some opt to become househusbands. Those men may have to endure feelings of invisibility, just as women have done. The threat can be especially intense if the man feels his role of unemployed or under-employed partner, or househusband, is scorned in his new community. But the opposite can be true too. He may be viewed as an intriguing pioneer, and attract special attention just because he is breaking a traditional mold.

Such men are still rare, whereas it is common for women to interrupt their work outside the home to follow their men. Their need to be recognized as individuals—separate from their role as someone's wife or lover or mother—comes sharply into focus after the move.

"When Martin comes home full of excitement and accomplishment, I feel angry," said Barbara, holding up her hands in a gesture of warding off, as though to push away her husband's satisfaction. "What have I accomplished here?" A professional photographer as well as a mother, Barbara had disrupted her career so that Martin could attend a distant law school. She would need to line up child care, organize a new studio, find new colleagues and clients, and locate a gallery to show her work before her identity as a photographer could again be affirmed.

For full-time homemakers, the challenge can be even greater. Their identities may have been composed of myriad roles both in and out of the home—tapestries of identity that unravel during a move. Functioning unseen within their new households, often viewed as agents to fill other people's needs, unknown as individuals outside the home, they are vulnerable to deep feelings of invisibility.

IDENTITY CONFLICTS

Some men think of their identities in a hierarchy of importance. It's not uncommon to hear men say, "My job has priority over my marriage." They may feel comfortable with that stance, since their identities in the workplace and their identities as financial providers for the family seem harmonious. Their relationships with their wives take second place.

Women are more likely to feel that their various identities have parallel importance. Barbara valued her identity as photographer—it expressed her talents and drew recognition from others. Yet she would have difficulty ranking her identities as wife, mother, and photographer on a vertical ladder. Those identities, and others she had developed in Iowa, were intertwined. When she moved, the whole tapestry came unraveled and had to be painstakingly reconstructed. This is a challenge for many movers, and during the reconstruction new doubts emerge.

"I can't visualize making the major commitment I need to be successful in a small and competitive field," said Liz, a specialist in Oceanic art. "I'm afraid you have to be selfish to make that commitment. Miles, my husband, seems quite selfish when he shuts everything out to concentrate on his research. I don't want to wall myself off, I want to be able to respond to people." A conflict between the ideal of achievement, approached through her identity as a scholar, and the ideal of personal connection, approached through her identity as a wife and best friend, raged within Liz.

"Since our move, I've felt crabby and irritable towards Miles," she said. "And I felt cold sexually. Here he is in a fine job and goes off to his office every day. I don't have that yet." Her painful feeling of invisibility was heightening her need for recognition outside the home, yet that wish was troubling her because professional work might compromise her capacity to respond to people she loved.

A conflict between caregiving and achievement outside the home tugs at many women and an increasing number of men. Settled people usually find temporary states of equilibrium between those aims, often planning their lives in phases. Moving may disturb the equilibrium and re-ignite the conflict.

NEW CLAIMS

That equilibrium may also be disrupted by new claims. The new employer can be a jealous spouse, demanding an intense involvement that interferes with personal relationships.

"Nobody knows what it's like; they wouldn't believe me," said Jane, the wife of a physician in training. "Derek is up by six and it's rare that he's home before seven. Every third night he's gone all night."

"When he comes home he's so exhausted and drained that he only wants to go to bed. There's so much I don't tell him about because he's too tired to deal with it. He can't even remember the things I do tell him." Medical training is one extreme example, but the expectation that the employer should be given priority pervades American society, and is heightened in periods when jobs are scarce. Few American institutions are as enlightened as those in Europe where practices such as flextime, job sharing, and parental leave recognize the importance of family relationships. The American mover can be caught in a no-exit conflict between the demands of the job and the needs of loved ones who may feel sad, lonely, envious, resentful, angry, and may seek solace in alcohol, food, or even in love affairs outside their marriage.

EMOTIONAL TANGLES

"You haven't talked about it this way before," Sylvia said in dismay, as she heard—really heard—about her husband's earlier distress.

"No, because I was worried about you, you were having a hard time carving out a life for yourself. And I'll tell you now, quite honestly I was sometimes pretty resentful that you were having such a hard time."

"So because you resented the way I was feeling, you closed off from me, was that it?"

"I guess so. But you seemed pretty closed off from me," said Scott. "I was afraid I'd made an awful mistake in accepting the job here."

"I thought I'd made an awful mistake in agreeing to come," said Sylvia. "But now—well, a lot of new realms have opened up in our lives."

"Would you want to go back?"

"No. You?"

"Not any longer."

Scanning their current lives, both realized that the move had spurred the development of new identities, even as the old were being reclaimed.

Scott and Sylvia's marriage was long-standing and resilient. Struggling through stormy times, they reached a deeper understanding of each other. For Jane and her husband, Derek, the outcome was grim—a breakdown of their marriage.

Within each couple, identity was a central issue. Both Scott and Derek had a professional identity that was respected in their new community, although the job stresses were severe. For Sylvia and Jane, there was a significant rupture of identity.

Jane was among the many women who move with partners involved in higher education or professional training, and who suppose that those three or five years will be a fine time to start a family. They will have a baby to love and be loved by, and a clear identity as a mother too. But with her partner absorbed in his work, the woman may in effect become a single parent, weary and confined by the baby's needs. Her loneliness and sense of invisibility can be heightened.

Jane had set aside her career in teaching to have her first child. Now she was surrounded by strangers, many who were stressed movers too, walling off their true feelings, showing smiling faces that served as barriers rather than links between them. In that setting, and with an absent or exhausted husband, she lacked the support she needed in her maternal role. Disappointment, frustration, and resentment simmered until the pot boiled over.

In contrast, Sylvia was gradually able to recreate her professional identity. Like other "following" partners, as she felt increasingly affirmed herself, she was better able to respond to her husband's needs.

HELPFUL STRATEGIES

PRESERVE YOUR PHYSICAL IDENTITY

The core of your identity is your physical self. Although moving gives you an opportunity to try out a new "look," that may involve too much change all at once. In the midst of strangeness, it is reassuring if the person reflected in the mirror every morning is the familiar you.

Consider what physical characteristic you're most eager to preserve. For many women, and an increasing number of men, it's hairstyle. In fact, hairstyle can feel so important that many movers travel back to their trusted hairdresser in the community they've left. If you can't afford the time or money to do that, try to notice haircuts you admire—among your colleagues, in the check-out line at the supermarket. Then, if the hair is paired with an amiable face, you might express your admiration and ask who does that person's hair. Most people will be flattered.

RECLAIM A MEANINGFUL ROLE

Women as well as men need to be visible outside of their homes. They need to show their capabilities and have them appreciated in their community. That is crucial to the positive adjustment of most movers.

It's easy to say to yourself, "I'll look into things as soon as I've finished unpacking and my home is settled." That's not a good strategy. It's far wiser to look back at your Lifescan (Chapter 2), and focus on a few roles that have been meaningful in the past. Then decide to activate them in your new life.

Some roles are dependent on other people. You can't play tennis without a partner. You probably won't want to cook Italian food without someone to share and enjoy it. But there are also roles you can carry out alone. You can swim alone, jog alone, critique paintings in a gallery alone. As you do it, you'll probably encounter others doing the same thing. Your identity as a jogger or bicyclist or cross country skier will be recognized, and you may begin to make connections with others on the track. Or in the art gallery.

You may want to "go public" intentionally. If one of your identities is "voracious reader," you could take out a library card, inquire about book discussion groups, and join one. If you're talented at piano, you might offer lessons. You might advertise your skills as a math tutor, freelance illustrator, or computer buff. If you have a knack with Greek pastries, you could sell them out of your home or at a local market. Before long, you'll be known as the person who makes the scrumptious baklava.

PACE YOURSELF

For some people, exploration and discovery are exhilarating. As movers, they want to go "all out" in investigating their new communities. And newcomers are often urged to throw themselves into a variety of new activities. That may cause an overload. There are three major reasons why it's wiser to monitor your pace.

First, it's easy to underestimate the amount of energy—both physical and emotional—that most moves involve. The tasks of re-creating a home, reclaiming your identity, and developing new friendships—along with doing your everyday work and tending your love relationships—are complex and tiring. Were you exploring a new place on a vacation, you might involve yourself intensely, knowing that at the end of a week or a month it would be over. But when you move, your time frame is much longer, and energy needs to be rationed.

"You have to be ready to give seventy-five percent and get twenty-five percent," cautioned an experienced single mover as she shared her wisdom about community involvement. That imbalance may be more than you can handle for many months after your move. So as you investigate groups of people who share common interests and work towards a common goal, consider saying, "I'm new, I'm interested in meeting people and learning about what you do, but I won't be able to make any commitments for a while."

The second reason for caution is this. Most salaried work involves reasonably clear expectations. In voluntary work, the boundaries are often ambiguous. The needs of voluntary organizations—whether Little League baseball, a political party, or a garden club—may seem limitless. It's often unclear how much involvement is enough for the organization or enough for volunteers to meet their own standards. So when you feel ready to take on an active role, try to keep it to a clearly defined minimum (two hours a week?) at first. It's easy to expand your role, but very hard to shrink it without disappointing others and yourself.

Third, it's important to decide whether you want to be viewed as a "professional volunteer"—a person whose entire commitment outside the home is on a voluntary basis. Such people have enormous value in community life, but that identity could get in the way of paid employment if you need it. If you offer your skills for free, why should you be paid? So think about your voluntary undertakings in terms of your future as well as your present. And do keep a record of your responsibilities for inclusion in a resume if you apply for paid work.

CLARIFY YOUR NEEDS

Although you may play numerous meaningful roles, there are probably two or three identities that feel central in your life. A move may change your priorities in ways that are confusing at first, even though the change leads to later growth.

Joan, for example, set aside her work as an occupational therapist when she married and moved to a new community for her husband's business training. Her goal was to become a nurturing wife and skillful homemaker. Her husband was able to support her financially, and he supported her emotionally in whatever roles she chose. Yet within months, she was searching unsuccessfully for a job, and her mood had plunged.

"I've felt worthless. I've cried a lot at night." Her renewed urge to be an occupational therapist had been fueled by her dual move—into a new community where she was not yet recognized and respected, and into a new marriage in which her dignity felt crucial.

"It's my need to have my part in the scenario," she explained. "Russell is growing, he's intellectually stimulated, he talks about what's happening to him. I want to be growing and experiencing and to have something to bring to the relationship." Clear now about her needs, Joan persisted in her search and found a job in her field. Her identity as a professional and her identity as a wife began enhancing each other.

Joan was able to discuss her dilemmas with her husband, her mother (in long distance phone calls), and an interviewer who was researching the impact of moving on women. If you feel confused about your priorities when you move, we urge you to call your best friend in the community you left, your brother or sister, your minister or rabbi—whatever people have understood you in the past. If you have a partner, turn to him or her and try to be open about your struggles, and encourage him or her to do the same.

PURSUE YOUR GOALS

Donna didn't subscribe to the Myth of the Transportable Homemaker—the myth that declares "I can be a wife and mother anywhere" (Chapter 2). When she moved, she realized that she would have to rebuild the infrastructure that helped her enjoy full-time mothering and homemaking.

She energetically gathered information about play groups that would provide playmates for her young children and companionship for herself. She did that by obtaining a list of nursery schools from the town library, phoning several and asking the registrars for information about play groups. She was given names of parents, and phoned them.

"It wasn't easy to make myself call strangers because I'm rather shy," she admitted. But the responses were friendly. They eased Donna into the next stage—visiting the groups that had openings, and noticing how other parents handled their children. She joined a group that felt compatible, and began arranging coffee times with women she wanted to know better. Ten months after her move, the group felt like a network of colleagues.

"It's nice to know that every week I'll be among women I'll be glad to see, and they'll be glad to see me." The women shared problems and solutions, comforted, encouraged, and validated each other.

If you are a full-time homemaker/parent, whether you're a mother or father, it will be crucial to establish your own parenting network.

If you're also employed outside your home, that will be more tricky because of the limits of your time and energy. But it can be done. For example, if your child is in day care or school, you may meet other parents who would welcome get-togethers in the evening or on weekends. Among them, or among your neighbors, you may be able to join or even start a baby-sitting cooperative.

Parents have significant identities outside of parenting. Other people have significant identities outside of their paid employment. One of the most important channels through which you can express and receive recognition of those other identities is within affinity groups. But since affinity groups also play a crucial role in establishing new friendships, we'll explore those possibilities in the next chapter.

Chapter 12 Exercises

Meaningful roles and identities will be lost when you move. You will want to reclaim some, but perhaps not all. This is a time to clarify your ideas about who and what you want to be in your new home, neighborhood, community, and/or workplace. So look again at your Lifescan in Chapter 2, and then begin these exercise.

EXERCISE A

Some of the roles you enjoyed in your previous home(s) included

_____

_____

_____

EXERCISE B

Now that you've moved, think for a moment about some of the different roles others expect you to play.

My partner counts on me to

_____

_____

My children/family count on me to

_____

_____

My friends count on me to

_____

_____

My boss/colleagues count on me to

_____

_____

Who else counts on you? For what?

_____

_____

EXERCISE C

Now that I've moved, my priorities include

_____

_____

_____

_____

EXERCISE D

Think about the roles you're expected to play, as well as the ones you've chosen for yourself. List below some of the resources you'll need (time? money? child care? information? special equipment? a friend or partner?) in order to fulfill each of these roles:

In order to be a _____, I need _____

_____

_____

In order to be a _____, I need _____

_____

_____

In order to be a _____, I need _____

_____

_____

In order to be a _____, I need _____

_____

_____

Think about what you'd like to be doing in the future as you answer these questions:

In a few weeks, I'd like to be _____

I'll need _____

_____

_____

In a few months, I'd like to be _____

I'll need _____

_____

_____

In a year, I'd like to be _____

I'll need _____

_____

_____

In two or three years, I'd like to be _____

I'll need _____

_____

_____

In five years, I'd like to be _____

I'll need _____

_____

_____

In ten years, I'd like to be _____
I'll need _____

_____

_____

Many years from now, I'd like to be _____
I'll need _____

_____

_____

When you've finished, you may want to show this exercise to your partner or a close friend. Talk over your goals with your partner or friend. Then encourage your partner to use the exercise too.

When I moved to this town I bought myself a dog to help me make friends.

Did it help?

Yes. A lot. It bit my neighbor — and now I'm dating the animal control officer.

CHAPTER 13

Dances of Friendship

DANCES OF FRIENDSHIP

Friendship is crucial to your well-being. It contributes significantly to both physical and mental health. It may even influence how long you live—some believe that one reason women's life expectancy is longer than men's is that women are more adept at forming deep friendships.

For women, intimate friendship is based on mutuality, spontaneity, authenticity, trust, and reciprocity. It is a confiding relationship in which each partner feels understood, valued, and supported

Some men develop confiding relationships too, but they tend to confide in women. It feels risky to expose their emotions and vulnerabilities to other men. Rather, they form male bonds by doing things together. As men live through shared experiences, those bonds may deepen, whether or not emotions are expressed in words.

For both men and women, it is slow going to develop new close friendships after a move. True, you'll experience an occasional "click" with someone you meet—the warming recognition that this person shares your interest and values, and may become a confiding friend. But instant intimacy rarely occurs. The relationship may become special, or it may not. You'll probably walk a tightrope, balanced between hope and disappointment, between attachment and loss. Growing friendships will cool when one or both discovers that you have less in common than you thought. Or the potential friend will promise to phone you and never follow through. Or s/he will take on new work and have little time or energy for getting together. Or s/he will move away.

You'll be caught up in a complex dance of friendmaking in which there will be advances, pauses, retreats, and painful falls. The bruises of rejection and disappointment will hurt. But if you expect progress to be slow, that realism may at least protect you from the bleak thought that there must be something wrong with you.

Most movers long to be reached out to as a first gesture of friendship. If you already have someone to act as your sponsor, reaching out may happen. Or if you move into a community with a strong tradition of welcoming newcomers, it may happen. Unfortunately, it also may not. Even a new workplace doesn't necessarily foster friendships.

"My colleagues were pleasant enough," said Ted, who moved to begin a new job in a high-tech firm. "But we all had separate offices. There wasn't even a staff room where people gathered for coffee, and nobody asked me to go out for lunch. It was efficient and impersonal, and I was lonely." In many workplaces like Ted's, electronic communication is reducing the number of face-to-face encounters. An E-mail letter is a poor substitute for a friendly smile.

It's been said that the opposite of love isn't hate. When there's hate, there's at least some involvement. The opposite of love is indifference. If your new community fails to hold out hands of friendship, you may feel lost in a cold, empty limbo of indifference. You may feel sad, lonely and scared. If there were a fire or an accident, who would help you? Who would sit with you in the hospital if your partner needed surgery? Whom would the school call if your child got sick and you weren't home?

HELPFUL STRATEGIES

One of your best sources of help is your own past experience. Before you read our ideas about making friends, look back at your Lifescan. Notice whom you identified as special people in your life. Try to recall how, when, and where you met those people, and what deepened those relationships. Think about the strategies you used and ask yourself whether any of them would be useful now.

REACHING OUT

If few people, or none, reach out to you after you've moved, it's up to you to seek out the early connections.

It sounds easy. Why not just talk to a stranger at a library, in the community pool, or on the street as you walk your dog? One reason you may hesitate is that you're unsure what kind of response to expect. There may be a friendly reaction, or there may be a cool rebuff.

"I walked over to see one of my neighbors. She came to the door but she didn't ask me in. She stood there and talked to me through the screen door. In Iowa, you would have people come in and you would feed them." This was Barbara the photographer's story, and she sounded appalled. The mesh of the screen door had been both a physical and psychological barrier that signaled, "Don't come too close."

In our violence-ridden society, many people have become wary of approaches by strangers. In our mobile society, many people are wary of forming attachments to newcomers who may soon move away again. Others are absorbed in their own lives, and don't have the time or energy to open the door to someone new. So you may be exposed to a lot of behavior that signals "don't come too close." Reaching out can be an emotionally draining effort.

Even if you've tried to learn about the culture of your new community (see Chapter 8), you may have discovered that there's a lot of ambiguity about what's expected from newcomers. Some people, especially women, are uneasy about taking the initiative in making new contacts. In part, this is because aggression is accepted as a masculine characteristic in our society but not as a feminine one. When women behave in ways that feel aggressive—taking the initiative often feels that way—they may be flooded with shame.

Too, they are uncertain about what the response will be. They fear they'll be seen as pushy, trying to worm their way into settled people's lives. And that may be true. Those whose lives are already overflowing may feel invaded by a needy newcomer.

Without guidelines to follow, it may be wise to make your first approaches to other newcomers (who are in the same boat). Your realtor or apartment building superintendent may be able to help you identify them among your neighbors, or the Welcome Wagon or Newcomer's Club may have a list.

If making a planned approach to a new person is too uncomfortable for you, try to locate the gathering places in the community. These are the places where people mingle informally, where repeated encounters happen spontaneously, where you will begin to recognize others and be recognized by them, where they and you will begin to smile at each other and say hello and, after a while, to chat for a few minutes. Short conversations may become longer, you may begin to show more of yourself and learn more about them. You may finally plan to get together.

The gathering places in your new community may be coffee houses or convenience stores, the salad bar in the supermarket, the parks, playgrounds, tennis courts, libraries, art galleries, museums, church parish houses. There are many possibilities, and they may change from time to time. And since they become known through word of mouth, you'll need to ask, ask, and ask—your neighbors, colleagues, clergy, librarians, teachers, and your health care providers.

Each time you make an outreaching gesture, you'll be risking emotional bruises. If you're a self-confident person who readily shrugs off rebuffs, we encourage you to make those gestures and take those risks. If you're a sensitive person who feels sad or angry when others turn away from you, you may feel safer making your approaches through groups that are already established.

AFFINITY GROUPS

Affinity groups are coalitions of people who share common interests and work towards common goals. They may be formal or informal, large or small, with programs that are highly structured or casually loose.

How can you find them? Some are probably listed in your phone book under Social and Human Services. Within that listing, there may be a few, such as a Women's Information Service, that can supply further information. The town hall or the public library may have directories of community organizations, or through the library you may have access to Internet.

The Welcome Wagon or Newcomer's Club is another source, and your realtor is too. If you are a member of a national organization, you could call or write the national office and inquire about branches in your new town. Meetings of special interest groups will probably be announced in the newspaper, or on bulletin boards in the library, church, school, or local store. Ask around to find out where notices are apt to be posted.

Since moving drains time and energy, you probably won't want to attend many gatherings at first. So try to clarify what you're searching for. Look back at your Lifescan again. Would a political organization, an environmental organization, a women's or men's group be interesting to you, or a musical group, a parenting network, a business association? Would it feel reassuring to turn towards the local chapter of a familiar national organization, or are you ready for something completely new?

If you feel shy about attending on your own—many people do—ask your partner, a neighbor who's offered help, or your teen-aged youngster to go to the first meeting with you.

Many groups are easy-going, but some are intense and on the lookout for new members ready to volunteer. It's wise to mention that you've come to learn about what the group is doing before you make a commitment to join. If you do join, it's wise to commit only a small amount of time until you see whether you want to invest energy here.

Finding your place in a group can be emotionally challenging, and it helps to be prepared for that. For example, people at a gathering may be distant and aloof, or they may be warm and friendly. But even if they're welcoming, you'll probably feel that you're at the margin for a while. You won't share in the common experience or the collective memory of the group—they'll talk about events and people you know nothing about. In many subtle ways, you may feel yourself being held outside, and that may reawaken sad memories of earlier times in your life when you were treated as an alien—the first cousin of E.T.

Furthermore, the members may welcome your talents but also feel threatened by them. Some people will fear that you'll outshine them, or take over their special place in the group. They'll feel competitive *with* you, and maybe also competitive *for* you. Sub-groups within the main group may jockey to pull you into an alliance with them, and oppose the aims of others. It may remind you of rivalries in your family or your school, and you may feel ill at ease.

If your discomfort is intense, why not withdraw for now and try a different organization instead? But if you're prepared for uncertainty and ready to work your way into the group gradually, you are likely to find the bonds strengthening. You'll begin to care about the others in the group. They'll begin to care about you.

As you notice people who might become close friends, try to create situations in which personal conversations can take place. Have a cup of coffee together after the meeting, or take a walk on another day. From the other person's response, you'll get an idea about whether s/he wants to pursue the relationship further. If s/he does, you'll be on the road towards friendship. But only on the road.

"I've been surrounded by friendly people but I've felt intensely lonely," a puzzled mover said. She was outreaching and involved with several affinity groups. But the contradiction in her experience was authentic. There are different forms of loneliness. Although she had developed social bonds, she still longed for the deep sharing of intimate friendship.

CONNECTIONS WITH OLD FRIENDS

Many movers feel that they can't be authentic among new people. They have to show a smiling face, irrespective of what they feel. They have to be cautious about disclosing their beliefs and values. In the words of one distressed mover, "With new people you're always having to prove yourself. I miss my dear friends intensely. They accepted me just as I am, good and bad."

So while new friendships are deepening—and that often takes several years—it's important to keep older friendships alive. If you can afford the time and money, plan visits to old friends. Or invite them to visit you. The phone is next best. Funds for long distance calls should be part of your moving budget.

It's warming to hear an old friend's voice and realize you can pick up the relationship where you left off. Or almost. You'll miss seeing your friend's face, you may miss the chance to hug each other. There may be a sense of estrangement, too. You and your friend no longer share your daily experience with each other—the small things that have big importance. Your friend may be angry at you for moving away. You may feel guilty because you did. Such feelings are common, and it helps if you can discuss them openly. You might make a comment something like this: "I feel as though something's coming between us. Let's figure out what it is." That signals your commitment to sustain the friendship, and, hopefully, your friend will make a commitment too.

But even so, when you hang up the phone, or when you finish reading a letter from your friend, sadness may surge up. Flow with it, if you can. It's part of grieving, and grieving is a necessary part of coming to terms with loss.

MONITOR YOUR FEELINGS

The work of making new friends can result in a clearer sense of who you are, and thoughtful choices about how and where you invest your time and energy. It can result in new relationships that enhance your life.

But you may experience a lot of emotional pain while friendships are developing. People will disappoint you and turn away from you. Their behavior will usually have nothing to do with you, but you may not feel sure of that. You may wonder anxiously if you're really a likable person. Memories of rejections in your past life may get churned up again, rekindling old resentment, sadness, and self-doubt.

Since you're feeling your way into new relationships, and you may not know what the local people expect, you'll probably make some blunders. Either because others react in a negative way, or because your behavior hasn't met your own standards, you may feel ashamed.

So, even if you wanted to move and are happy you've done it, it's likely that you'll also feel sadness, longing, anger, anxiety, guilt, and shame. You may experience those painful emotions before you move, right after you've moved, or many months later—that varies from one person to the next. The emotions are likely to ebb and flow, sometimes welling up and catching you off guard, and then subsiding and leaving you feeling content again.

When they do surge up, remind yourself that they're common among movers, and they don't signify that you're inadequate or peculiar. Try to comfort and replenish yourself (see Chapter 11). Turn to someone you trust and talk about those feelings.

Be mindful that there are danger signs. If you feel anxious all the time, and begin having physical symptoms such as shaky hands, rapid breathing, a pounding heart, sweating, and if you have repeated nightmares, those are danger signs. If you feel persistently tired and hopeless, if you lose interest in your work and feel irritable with your partner or children, if your appetite and sleep patterns are different than usual, and—above all—if you feel that you're a worthless person and begin thinking about suicide, those are danger signs.

They are signs that you need to seek out a qualified mental health clinician—a clinical social worker, a psychologist, a psychiatrist, or a pastoral counselor. If you have a new health care provider, you can ask for a referral. If not, you can inquire through the mental health center or family service agency listed in your phone book. Your employer or your partner's employer may have an EAP (employee assistance program), with a counselor who can supply you with names.

A careful clinician will start with an evaluation of your difficulties, and a recommendation as to whether psychotherapy, either with or without appropriate medication, would be helpful. If you have physical symptoms, s/he should urge you to have a medical examination too.

There are still many mental health clinicians who underestimate the powerful impact of moving. Before you go for your first interview, it can be helpful to review the range of losses you have experienced, and try to clarify your thoughts about the most stressful aspects of reconnecting.

Chapter 13 Exercises

EXERCISE A

Making new friends after a move is rewarding but also complicated and disturbing. The following exercises will help you think about the strategies that can work best for you.

Who are the friends you miss the most right now?

Who? _____

Why? _____

Who? _____

Why? _____

Who? _____

Why? _____

Who? _____

Why? _____

In what ways are you keeping in touch with some of your friends?

_____

_____

_____

_____

If you're not keeping in touch, what are your reasons?

_____

_____

_____

_____

Now think about some of the ways that people have let you know that they wanted to develop a friendships with you. List some of those friendly gestures below.

_____

_____

_____

_____

How did you respond to some of those gestures?

_____

_____

_____

_____

Think about some friendly gestures you have made to others to let them know that you wanted to become friends.

_____

_____

_____

_____

How did other people respond to your friendly gestures?

_____

_____

_____

_____

Now think about some friend-making gestures you used in the past. What are some friendly gestures that were easy for you to make?

_____

_____

_____

_____

What are some friendly gestures that you've made, even though they felt pretty risky?

_____

_____

_____

_____

What are some friendly gestures you've thought about making, but decided not to because they just feel too risky?

_____

_____

_____

_____

What are some of the places where you've met and made friends in the past?

_____

_____

_____

_____

What are some of the places where you've tried unsuccessfully to meet and make new friends?

_____

_____

_____

_____

Now that you've moved, what are some of the places in your new community where people you might like seem to gather?

_____

_____

_____

_____

EXERCISE B

You'll need your journal again for this exercise. Every day, write about the things you did that day to take care of yourself.

CHAPTER 14

Helping Your Youngsters Grow New Roots

"You want to interview me about what I did to help my kids through the move?" Lynn sounded amazed. "I didn't do anything right. I did it all wrong! Nobody tells you how to move, you're just supposed to know."

Parents are "just supposed to know," but how can they if they've never done it? Or if they've moved without children, or with children at different ages? They can't. We hope our ideas, gathered from many movers, will help. We'll suggest ways to help youngsters loosen their ties to places and people they've had to leave and then develop attachments to new ones.

🏠

We don't know if Lynn asked for help when she felt bewildered. Many women don't. Many women take on the sole responsibility for helping children settle into new homes, new neighborhoods, new day-care centers and schools, new friendships. Many women expect themselves to observe, care, worry, listen, and solve problems as they watch their children expressing not only excitement and happiness about a move, but also sadness, fear, confusion, loneliness and hurt. They ask themselves to make it come out right for the family. But that's too heavy a burden to carry alone.

FOR SINGLES

If you're a single parent, who might you turn to? Who helped you prepare your children for your move? Could you turn back to that person, at least on the phone? Could you ask that person to make a visit soon?

If a new neighbor or colleague asks, "Is there any way I can help?" you might say, "I'm worried about the kids and I'd love to talk it over." Or ask that person to give you a time-out by tending the children for a few hours.

You might search out a support group for parents of children who've moved through the Newcomer's Club, the Employee Assistance Program in your place of employment, the church or synagogue you plan to attend, or through your child's new school. If there's no support group in place, ask if there are people who would act as informal advisors about helping new children get settled. Many schools now have "class parents" who could make suggestions. Or your community may have a Retired and Seniors Volunteer Program (RSVP), and there may be seniors who would enjoy sharing your experience or being a proxy grandparent to your child.

FOR COUPLES

Women often protect their male partners after a move, saying, "He's new at his job and very stressed. I don't want to bother him with what the kids are going through." If you're a househusband and your wife is the breadwinner, you may feel the same way. But it's risky to assume your partner doesn't want to hear about the children. He (the chief breadwinner is still usually the man) may be worried about them. If you close him out, he may feel useless or helpless as a parent, and you may feel dumped on and resentful. If you don't talk about your worries, they'll leak out in other ways—an irritable edge to your voice, a thunderous look on your face.

If you share your concerns with your partner, you're giving him a chance to feel effective as a parent during the time when he may not yet feel effective in his workplace. But be thoughtful about how and when you approach him. Rather than blurting out your fears when he comes through the door—although you're tempted—it works better to try something like this: "It upsets me to see how the kids are behaving and feeling, and I'd really like to talk it over with you. When would be a good time?" Your partner may respond with a vague "later," and you may need to persist: "Would you rather talk after dinner or after the kids are in bed?" Most partners will accept a choice that offers a sense of control.

When you talk about the children, try to include some of the positive things you've noticed—maybe your child has finally been invited to play at a school friend's house. Both of you need to focus on what's going well in addition to what's been a disaster.

When you discuss the problems ("John cries every morning and says he hates his new teacher"), suggest specific ways you'd like help from each other. You might say, "John's having trouble with math. It would help if you could spend time every evening checking his homework, then maybe play a game with him." Too, ask each other for ideas about how each of you could help.

It's easy to feel guilty if your children are having hard times and you're the parent who uprooted them. Sharing that feeling with your partner can make it easier to bear. Hiding it may cause it to intensify.

Naturally, you're eager for your children to adjust quickly. You want them to be happy, and you want reassurance that the move hasn't harmed them. But it's wise to lower your expectations for a while. Children need time to feel at home in a new place, and make new friends. And many children slump in their school performance the first year after a move. Be patient, remembering that it means a lot to your children when you show your support and concern. It means a lot for them to see their parents working together to help them.

Finally, if you're stressed by the children, remember the oxygen mask (Chapter 9)! You and your partner need to ask each other for time-outs from caring for the children. And you need to keep monitoring how you're both taking care of yourselves and each other.

FEELING AT HOME

SETTLING IN

For a young child, home is the center of the universe. It's a cocoon of safety and familiarity. Even in the first year of life, infants notice and respond to changes in what they see, hear, smell, taste, and touch. For example, Sue showed distinct reactions to her move at nine months (see Chapter 3).

"When we got there, she was actually looking for her things," said Judy, her mother. "She was beginning to kind of talk and she was pointing and she got very irritable. So the first thing I did after we unloaded the truck, I set up her room like it was at home, and then I propped her in the middle of the room, and until I did I think she was sort of anxious. She really needed to see her crib, her bookshelf and her stuffed animals."

"We moved back when she was twenty-two months old and she was upset to see me pack up her toys. I reminded her that they were coming with us, and the first thing I did when we got here was to get her room set up again. She needed that to get her bearings."

Sue was highly responsive to her surroundings and, fortunately, had a mother who understood. Judy gave priority to re-creating Sue's cocoon. That's an excellent strategy with a baby. But with a young child, there's more to it than that.

Ellen, too, knew that familiar furniture and toys contribute to a young child's sense of security—in the child's mind, those special objects are links to the people who give care and love. So Ellen, too, tried to recreate swiftly a nucleus of home for her two-and-a-half-year-old son, Ralph, when they moved. But her efforts backfired.

"I put him in day care for a whole day—I wanted to get his room ready right off. When I brought him home, he didn't want to go in, he seemed completely confused. He kept asking how it got there. I realized he couldn't understand how his room appeared in a different place. He needed to see how it happened, who carried the boxes, what they looked like. He needed to look into a moving truck."

Perhaps the crucial difference between Ralph's's experience and Sue's was that she was directly involved in the process, watching her parents unload their moving truck, watching her mother set up her new room, even "helping" in simple ways. That involvement could have turned the abstract idea of "moving" into a real experience.

But right through the pre-school years, a new apartment or house can seem scary.

"When we got to our new place," Nancy remembers, "I went in and raced from room to room to see MY new house, I was so excited. Then I brought the twins inside—they were three. The mess of cartons upset them, but we sat down together and opened the moving boxes they had packed. Once they had some familiar toys, they seemed more relaxed."

"I began to walk around the house, imagining how to put our home together. Every time I left the twins alone they began to scream, 'mommy, where are you?' That went on for four or five days—they followed me from room to room, carting a few favorite toys."

In spite of Nancy's sensitive parenting, her twins were anxious. It's common for young children to react to confusing changes with babyish behavior—fussing, clinging, disturbed sleep, losing new-found skills like feeding themselves, or using the toilet.

Such reactions usually pass in a few weeks if you can be responsive and reassuring. Unfortunately, they happen while you're feeling the strains of moving yourself, and it is hard to be patient. Now's the time to ask for support from your partner or close friend. If you're very worried about your children, talk over their reactions with their health care provider, even if it's a consultation by long distance phone.

Even for older children, a new place may feel alien.

"One night my husband and I heard a really strange noise, like ripping," Nora told us. "I found my teen-aged daughter ripping the wallpaper off her walls. She got the room with the football wallpaper on it, and we didn't change it because we're just renting. Peg said she wanted plain white walls. Y'know, I wasn't mad at her—I felt bad. I thought that room would be good for her because it was the biggest."

Maybe Peg's mom could have given her more of a voice in the allocation of rooms, rather than deciding what would be good for her. But Peg may have been showing that she wasn't ready to feel at home in the new house. Youngsters need to detach themselves emotionally from their previous homes before they can attach to the new.

SAYING GOOD-BYE TO YOUR OLD HOME

"In our move when Ralph was two and a half, he even missed the bugs!" Ellen remembered. "He wanted to make a dozen trips back to our old house—fortunately it wasn't too far. At first, he wanted to go in the house, then peak through the window, then finally just drive past to say good-bye."

"The strange thing I've noticed with Polly, she's six, is that she refuses to look at our old house," said Lynn. "We drive by every time we go into the city and I love to see it, but Polly hasn't looked at it since we moved—she kind of puts her head down and hides her eyes. She told us she'll never look at it because it makes her too sad. When we moved, she was really sad. We'd talked about it for months and she saw the new house lots of times. Then it really happened and I think she just felt shock that we took her away from her home."

There's a difference between the idea of moving and the reality. Preparation enhances a child's self-confidence, but it doesn't prevent emotional reactions. When the reality sinks in, your youngsters will probably feel sad. If you're happy about your move, your children's feelings can be hard to understand. If you're grieving too, you may be afraid that your children's sadness will start you crying. Or if the children's sadness makes you feel guilty about uprooting them, it may be hard to tolerate. For any of those reasons, you may want to disqualify the sad feelings: "Our new house is much nicer than our old one," or to paper them over: "Cheer up, we'll go to the mall and do some shopping." Then your children may feel not only sad but lonely in their sadness, too.

Keep in mind that grief is a healthy response to loss. Remember that grief isn't *all* your children are feeling. For example, during the time when Polly was refusing to look at her old home, she was also expressing pleasure about her new school. And remember that the grief will pass. Polly told her mother that when she grew up she would buy her old home and live in it with friends. Even in her sad mood, she was hopeful about the future.

It helps your children if you allow them to grieve, comforting them with a lap or an arm around their shoulders. You can help by letting them express their sadness in words, maybe asking what they're missing about their previous home. You might suggest that they make drawings of their previous homes, or look at photos with you (they may not want to while the feelings are too raw). You might plan to make a visit.

The grieving is likely to take time. But while it's happening, new connections are forming, too.

RE-CREATING THE SENSE OF HOME

"I love to garden," said Jill, "and we planted some plants in our yard—ones that I had dug up from our last house. We had a little ceremony in our new yard, and I talked to the kids about starting over, and how the plants would grow here just like we would, too. Then we talked about doing the same thing with a tree! So we drove back, got a tree from the woods near our house, and planted it in our new yard. It was a real ceremony, and it helped us accept that it was time to live here."

You may have your own ideas about rituals of connection. Why not ask your children for theirs?

There are other ways to foster a sense of connection. If you don't know what possessions help your youngsters feel linked to important people and places, why not ask them? Then work with them to restore the things they need—maybe certain toys for pre-schoolers, maybe a hi-fi system for a teenager.

You may feel, as Ellen did, that your new place is MY house. But try to give your children some choices in arranging their own rooms and recreation spaces, and involve them in the actual doing. Their ideas may not be the same as yours, but there will be opportunities for changes later. Right now, you're helping them feel they have some control over their new environs. And by encouraging self-expression, you're fostering a sense of belonging.

Familiar routines and rhythms are comforting. In the midst of change, it's reassuring to know that life is still predictable in certain ways—the family will gather around the dinner table or go on a Saturday excursion. Too, it's reassuring when there are clear rules about behavior, although a little extra flexibility is helpful after a move. If there's too much tussling about picking up their rooms, the new apartment or house won't feel like a very safe haven.

Home includes your neighborhood and community too. Family outings, even brief ones, are fine ways to begin exploring. After you've located the essentials—food store, gas station, bank, post office—why not begin searching for the kinds of places that have really mattered in the past? You might take turns deciding what to hunt for—a hill that looks right for sledding, a cafe that serves blueberry muffins, a video rental store. Look back at your Lifescans to remind yourselves of each person's special places.

Finally, keep in mind that a new place is neither safe nor familiar at first. It may be physically dangerous, with stairs to tumble down, objects to trip over, poison ivy in the woods, an open pond nearby. Show the children how to call 911. Accidents are common among movers.

🏠

MISSING SPECIAL PEOPLE

From early childhood, youngsters form deep attachments to caregivers, playmates, teachers, and close relatives. When they realize that they won't be seeing favorite people on a regular basis—or maybe ever again—they're likely to feel intensely sad.

For pre-school children, with limited understanding of time and distance, the sadness is probably mingled with confusion.

"When Ralph was two and a half, we moved away from the town where my brother lived," Ellen recalled. "The kids had seen their Uncle Rudi every day. After we moved, we phoned Rudi about once a week. Ralph had very animated conversations with him, but he always cried after we said good-bye. He told me he missed his uncle. At first, I wondered if we should call less often since the calls upset him so much, but I really knew he needed the contact—and the chance to express his sadness."

"Ralph was confused by the distance. Sometimes he'd say, 'Mommy, let's go to Rudi's house and pick raspberries,' as we were getting into the car to go to market. I'd have to explain that our houses were far away, and we'd have to plan a trip and pack some clothes and toys in our suitcases. We did go for visits, but it was hard for Ralph to understand why they couldn't be frequent and spontaneous."

In Ellen's shoes, many parents would have stopped the phone calls, and talked with their relatives after the child was in bed. She recognized that young pre-schoolers aren't sure that people who are out of sight really continue to exist—that understanding develops during the first three years of life. The phone calls reassured Ralph that his uncle hadn't stopped existing, and could still be a part of Ralph's life. Too, she understood that Ralph needed to feel and express his sadness. Many children his age have trouble talking about feelings like "I miss my uncle." They can only show their sadness in tears and behavior that may mystify their parents.

You can help your children deal with their grief if you talk about people who have been special in their lives. Bring out photographs, too. They may prompt an outburst of tears that upsets you. But it's healthy for young children to release and then understand their feelings. As you comfort your child, you might say, "I think you're sad because we're so far from Uncle Rudi." If you're sad too, it's helpful to say so: "I miss Uncle Rudi. I feel like crying, too." If it's realistic, reassure your child that you will see that special person again.

Pets can be beloved members of the family. For reasons of age, health, or quarantine regulations, pets may have to be left behind or "put down" when a family moves. Those separations have to be grieved, too. There will be sadness, tears, longing, and memories to be shared.

Older children who move can talk about sadness and longing more easily if they know it's acceptable (the ideas we've offered for dealing with grief in Chapters 7 and 11 may help). But missing special people has a dimension that missing special places doesn't have—the people who've been left behind have feelings, too. Those feelings may make it complicated to stay connected.

STAYING CONNECTED

Very young children can stay connected to special people by sending and receiving photos and drawings. School-age children can be encouraged to send postcards and write letters too. If you haven't already enlisted the help of your children's former teachers, why not drop them a note? Explain that your children will be writing to classmates, and ask the teacher to encourage them to write back. Some teachers will post your children's new address in the classroom. Some teachers will write a note themselves.

From the time that they can carry on a conversation, youngsters can talk on the phone. Find out when the lowest rates apply and agree on the frequency and length of calls (don't let your guilt about moving spur you to allow youngsters to run up a phone bill you can't afford).

Some of your children's friends may feel angry as well as sad because you left them, so they may not respond in a positive way. Be alert to that possibility. If your children are not getting answers to their cards or letters, or if they're not only sad after a phone call but maybe confused or resentful, too, it could help to say something along these lines: "When people's friends move away, they usually feel sad, but they're sometimes angry, too, because the move had to happen. Do you think Amy's angry?"

Your children may ask to visit a relative or friend, or to have that person visit you. If it's not possible, you may feel frustrated, and your own distress about the separation can be stirred up again. It's easy to be dismissive: "I've already told you! John is too far away now and we won't see him again until summer." Unfortunately, a response like that belittles your child's longing. It's more constructive to say, "Whenever you ask to visit Anne it makes me think about her and how much I'd like to see her, too. What do you like most to do with her?" An answer like that encourages your children to talk about the positive meanings of relationships, as well as the sadness of loss. If a visit is a reasonable possibility, you can start making plans together.

CONNECTING WITH NEW PEOPLE

PRE-SCHOOL CHILDREN

If you have full-time employment, the most important new people for your pre-schooler will be child care providers. You may have lined up some possibilities before you moved. If not, here are some places to begin your search: The EAP office at your employer and your partner's employer; the school secretary at the elementary school your child will attend later (s/he may know of good caregivers, or may be able to give you names of school parents who have pre-schoolers in day care); the Newcomer's Club or other organization for newcomers in the community; the church you plan to attend; the physician and/or nurse who will provide health care for your child; your new neighbors.

Try hard to arrange with your employer, or your partner's employer, that one of you will delay starting full-time work until your youngster is settled into new day care. At least, try to arrange for some flexibility of hours. Pre-schoolers are readily overwhelmed when too many major changes happen at once. While your little one is dealing with the strangeness and confusion of being in a new home, s/he will probably be clingy and more upset by separation from parents than usual. S/he is likely to need extra reassurance and soothing.

It helps if the child care provider maintains your child's usual routine as much as possible. And beloved stuffed animals, favorite story books, music, and toys are reassuring.

What about playmates? If you're an at-home parent, you may need them more than your child. Here's why. For their first three years, children enjoy each other's company, but they engage in "parallel play." That is, they may be absorbed in play alongside other children, but there's little real interaction with each other. It's when children are three and four that they flourish among playmates in nursery school or play groups.

But when your children are infants and toddlers, *you* need interaction to feel supported in your role as parent (see Chapter 12). You need to be among other parents with whom you can share your interests, accomplishments, and worries.

Where to find them? You might call nursery schools and ask if they could put you in touch with parents interested in playdates for preschoolers. Organizations for newcomers may run daytime activities for parents, with child care provided (they may also run evening activities for parents who are employed full time). Libraries and bookstores offer story hours for pre-schoolers and their parents. Also, the town hall or League of Women Voters may publish a directory of community resources, including facilities for parents and children.

Then start exploring, with your little one as your companion. Walk around your neighborhood and introduce yourself to people outside. Go to the places where parents gather with young children—the playground, swimming pond, sledding hill, science museum, ice cream shop.

If you're an outgoing person, it can be fun to strike up conversations with other parents who look friendly. But if you're shy, it may not feel like fun. In fact, many women feel uncomfortable in strange surroundings without an adult companion. You may want to enlist a new neighbor or acquaintance who has said, "Let me know if there's anything I can do," and ask that person to go exploring with your child and you.

At times, newcomers feel rebuffed when they try to make contacts.

"People weren't as responsive as I expected," said Judy, recalling her move when Sue was almost two. "I don't know if it's this town, or if it's just that mothers of small children are so tired, but I found that people were not even quite making eye contact. I'd go to the park and I'd say,' Oh, Sue, look, there's a little girl.' We'd start playing and I'd, like, try to make eye contact with the mother and she wouldn't even look at me."

If something like this happens to you—it's disappointing and hurtful when it does—try to keep in mind that it's not a personal reaction to you. The other woman may be exhausted, she may be depressed, she may need her privacy. So turn to your partner or a close friend for comfort and encouragement, and then go out and try again

ELEMENTARY SCHOOL-AGE CHILDREN

School will be at the center of your children's new lives. Hopefully, you made contact with their new school while you were preparing for your move (Chapter 9). If you arrive in the new community before the school year starts, give the school secretary a call quite soon. Ask if there's an orientation program for incoming students and parents. If there isn't, try to arrange an informal visit when your children and you can meet the principal and, possibly, your children's new teachers. If they're not available during the summer, have a look at the classrooms, the library, the cafeteria, and the playground so that your children will have some sense of familiarity on their first day. A momentous day!

"The second day after we moved was a big one for Ralph," wrote Ellen, after moving again when Ralph was seven. "He was going to start at his new school. In the morning he asked for a haircut! So I gave him one—he obviously wanted to look good. We walked to school, and I went in to meet his teacher. Ralph was quiet, and I sensed he was scared. Then the children began coming. Fourteen kids walked in calling out, 'Hi, Ralph!' I noticed the same numbness I saw in Ralph before we moved. He didn't respond to anyone, and seemed close to tears, but he told me I could go."

"Walking home, I thought about how hard this was for Ralph. I couldn't wait for him to come home, but at the end of the day he was fine, he'd had a good time at school. Except for recess. 'I just walked around all by myself.' THAT got to me, and I started feeling awful about moving."

"Over the next few days, Ralph came home with the same report: 'School is good, but I have no one to play with at recess.' It broke my heart to see how lonely and sad he was feeling."

"I suggested inviting other kids over after school, but Ralph didn't want to. I suggested that he call up some of his old friends just to say 'hi.' He didn't want to do that either. He was in some sort of social limbo, and went on being very sad. One morning, after about a week of school he said, 'I like going to school, but it's kind of hard because I don't have any friends, and I'm used to having friends.' I wondered again if moving had been the right choice, but I was feeling so good myself—all the things I want in my life are here. What an irony! The move that made my life better has turned Ralph's life upside down."

"I have ideas about what was happening. Ralph was really grieving for the friends he'd left, the school he'd left, and the other pieces of his life that are so far away now. He needed time to feel his losses, and he seemed to know it. However, in my panic ('Oh no, he has no friends, and it's all because I wanted to move') I started to push him through his sadness and into making new friends faster than he could go."

"I think I was able to control my panic and guilt fairly quickly because I like it here, and Ron was around to give me a lot of support. I could listen better to Ralph because I felt safe and cared for myself."

"Then, one day, Ralph came home from school full of stories about his new friend, Mike. It had taken him a couple of weeks to recover from the shock of being the new kid and to work through some of his grief, and then he was ready to make a new friend. Now he's sailing! He and Mike, the two new kids, have started a Monster Detective club, and now all the kids are playing together at recess."

Some school-age children settle into their new lives quickly and happily. They like their teachers, they make friends easily and are accepted in school, neighborhood, and community groups. Perhaps the academic work in their new schools is similar to what they did in their previous schools (it might be easier), and they feel smart, successful, and well liked by classmates and teachers.

It's usually not that smooth. Some youngsters find it hard to make friends—their confidence suddenly vanishes. Like Ralph, they may not immediately be ready for new friendships. Or their classmates may not be ready to take them in. There may be cliques and teams that are difficult to break into. There may be youngsters who bully and tease—in fact, it's common for newcomers to be the target of teasing. Unsupervised, unstructured times like recess can be dismal interludes when newcomers walk around feeling embarrassed, rejected, ignored, and may even be shoved, pinched, or hit for no cause other than being new. New teachers may be more permissive than the ones youngsters had before, leaving them feeling confused. Or the teachers may be stricter. They may assign more classwork and homework than the children are used to.

For any of these reasons, when your kids come home from school and you greet them with, "Hi, how did it go?" it's likely that you'll hear some tales of woe. They may be repeated for days, weeks, or even months.

MORE WAYS YOU CAN HELP

· Listen to your child. S/he needs to feel understood and supported. This may be hard, since your child's distress may cause you to feel as guilty as Ellen felt. Or you may be struggling with sadness and loneliness of your own. To foster communication, you might put that into words: "I feel really bad that you're having a hard time because we moved," or "I'm having a hard time being new, just like you." Then make it clear that you care a lot about how your child is feeling, and that, together, you'll try to figure out solutions to the problems.

· Ask children for their ideas about how problems might be solved, and then ask how they think their parents could help. At that point, you'll probably want to offer your own ideas. For example, maybe your child has been teased. Since children being teased often feel powerless to stop it, point out that there are different ways your child could respond: ignore the teaser, cry, tell the teacher, just feel angry and hurt, tell the teaser to stop. Decide together which would be the best response to try. If the teasing persists, you might propose talking to the teacher yourself.

· Make sure your children don't come home to an empty apartment or house. If your employment schedule makes it impossible to be home when your child returns from school, try to find a baby-sitter through the high school, your neighbors, or your church. Tell the sitter that the youngster will need extra interest and support until s/he stops feeling new.

· Encourage your child to make active choices. For example, s/he and you might lay out clothes for the next day together, talking about what your youngster has noticed the other kids are wearing. If your child is intensely attached to something you think should be recycled, try to understand the meanings it has. Does it remind him of his buddies at the school he had to leave? Is it soft and cozy, and helps her feel safe?

· Enlist the help of the school.

First, collaborate with your child's teacher. Ask whether another child has been assigned as a "special friend" to shepherd your child through the period of being new. Ask for the teacher's observations about your child: Is s/he isolated or sociable at school? Is there a particular child your child seems compatible with? Ask the teacher for ideas about handling special problems.

Second, find out if there is a class parent. Call that person and ask about the class, the school, and activities in the community that your child might enjoy. Ask about the culture of the community. For children, that's expressed in certain styles of haircuts, clothing, styles of bikes, and recreational systems like Nintendo and Sega Genesis. Feeling in sync with other youngsters is intensely important to school-age children. It may boost your child's confidence to wear an "in" type of t-shirt.

Ask the class parent for names of other parents who've recently moved. They may have good ideas about ways you could help your child.

Third, find out which of your child's classmates live near your new home. You may get that information from the school directory, the school secretary, the teacher, or the class parent.

· Help your child get involved.

First, keep in mind that it's common for children who have moved to feel shy. Since trying to make friends in a class of twenty–thirty children can seem overwhelming, arrange a few play dates with just one or two classmates—someone your child has talked about, or someone the teacher has suggested. Don't push it; wait until your child feels ready. If s/he isn't interested the first time you suggest it, wait a week or two and then bring it up again.

This time, frame your suggestion differently. If your child feels shy about a one-on-one playtime with another child, you might suggest including that child in a family outing. Or plan an activity with the family of your child's classmate or another family in your neighborhood.

Second, get your youngster involved in after school activities. That will offer a way of being among other youngsters and also help your youngster reclaim an identity. But be sensitive to which identity your youngster wants to reclaim. Does s/he have a special skill or talent? Has s/he previously enjoyed dance classes, or team sports? Would s/he like to try out a new sport or hobby? Check the local Y and community recreation center for good programs at reasonable cost.

Keep in mind that children need "downtime" too. Many youngsters are overscheduled with stimulating activities. They need time without expectations—hopefully, not always near the TV. They need time for daydreaming, experimenting, hanging out. They need quiet time with you.

ADOLESCENTS

In the midst of rapid physical changes, teenagers can be intensely self-conscious. There are myriad sources of embarrassment—being conspicuous, making a mistake, being different from their age mates in height, clothing, hairstyle, skin color, or in being a newcomer.

By now, the responses of peers are as important as the responses of parents in shaping a youngster's sense of self. Peers support teenagers as they struggle to feel distinct from their families, to clarify their own values, and to make independent choices about their lives. Peers confirm their worth, and thus strengthen their self esteem—or they cast doubt on their worth and erode their self-esteem. Their influence is strong.

As they support each other, sometimes bonding against adult authority, teens often close ranks against outsiders. They form tight cliques and gangs which may be cruelly rejecting towards newcomers who try to break in. Sometimes the rejection is expressed through teasing, sometimes by ignoring or even refusing to speak.

Teens live in the moment. Without the longer range perspective of adulthood to help them absorb a rebuff or disappointment, their reaction is likely to be intense.

For these four reasons, making new friends is intensely important and risky for adolescents who move.

HOW CAN PARENTS HELP?

· Ensure that your teenagers are placed in appropriate classes, verifying that their school records were received by the new school.

· Encourage your youngsters to participate in orientation sessions, and urge them to learn about the bus route, and the location of lockers, classrooms, gyms etc. so they won't feel conspicuous or incompetent.

· Make certain they know how to reach one parent during the day.

· If they have special health needs, make sure the school nurse and guidance counselor are informed.

· Help your teenagers get in sync with the culture of the new school. Ask them what they notice about clothing, hairstyle etc., and then help them get to Main Street or the mall to find some emblems of local style.

· Consider your style of communicating. The principles of good communication that we've discussed in relation to younger children apply with teenagers, too. But there are differences. Adolescents are likely to be more protective of their private worlds of thought and feeling, Direct questioning is rarely fruitful. But it can help to have times when you and your teen take a walk or jog together, or go for a bike ride or a drive. Motion can dispel some of the intensity, and your youngster doesn't have to catch your eye. You can set an example by talking honestly about some of your own feelings about being a newcomer—both the sunny side and the shadow side.

You'll want to reassure your teenager that things will get better, but some teens hear that as a dismissal of their feelings. And you can't really know when or how much things will improve. It's more useful to point out that many teens have tough times when they move. Then remind your youngster that you'll help to brainstorm problems.

Your teenagers may be quite angry at you or your partner for causing the move. It's not easy, but it's helpful if you can convey understanding. It's healthier for your youngsters to talk about anger than to express it in destructive behavior.

• Help your teenagers widen their social sphere. It is hard to make new friends during the school day. Classes are tightly scheduled, and there's too much commotion at lunch. So extracurricular activities are the most likely source. Encourage your teens to identity all their interests and talents. Would they prefer to resume an activity that was satisfying before you moved, or is this the time to try something new and develop a new identity? They, not you, should choose what they'll try, although it's reasonable to ask them to make a commitment for at least a couple of months.

Just by being a newcomer, your youngster is an outsider. if s/he is different in another way—a member of a racial, ethnic, or religious minority group, or a youngster with a health impairment—that's double indemnity. Using all the resources we've mentioned, you'll need to find out and inform you teenager about support groups as well as special recreational facilities s/he might need. For example, there are now outstanding programs for physically challenged young athletes. If you can't have a constructive conversation with your teens about their choices, ask your partner, a close friend or relative, or the school guidance counselor to give it a try. Too much empty time puts a teenager at risk. Many a youngster first tries alcohol or drugs because "There's nothing else to do," and because the kids at the margin—the substance abusers in or out of school—may be the most receptive to a newcomer.

The lonely, anxious, angry state of feeling like an outsider can make teens more vulnerable to intense infatuations too. Direct parental opposition to a romantic coupling usually backfires, but two things can be done. First, even if you favor abstinence, make certain that your teens understand how to protect themselves from pregnancy and disease. Second, continue your efforts to help them make new friends.

Sometimes a new family can act as a catalyst in a neighborhood—giving a pancake party on a snowy weekend, organizing a Fourth of July cookout for the whole block. Neighbors whose lives have drifted apart can mingle, eat, laugh, and renew their acquaintance. A gathering like that is likely to include teenagers, or parents of teenagers who could help your youngsters make connections.

· Plan family excursions. The weeks or months until your teenager has made friends provide a special opportunity for family outings. You might put up a big calendar and encourage everyone to write in their ideas. Later, when your youngsters are fully involved, and your own evenings are absorbed with social and community doings, you'll all look back at those excursions with nostalgia.

WHEN THINGS DON'T GO WELL

"I shouldn't have promised the kids that we'd have their friends from Philadelphia come to visit," said Jill eighteen months after her move. "I was so overwhelmed with the house and the boxes that I didn't want to have all those kids around. Mine were really mad at me, and they didn't want to have anything to do with the kids here. It was awful. I told them I was sorry for promising, but I couldn't drive down to get their old friends."

"My ten year old still has no friends here—he never wants to invite anyone over, and he has no friends at school. He told me he hated me and his dad, he wanted to go home again. He actually screamed at me: 'You forced us to move, it wasn't my idea!'"

"How did I react? I said, 'I'm glad you're telling us how you feel.' He had all those feelings pent up and they had to come out. I knew that he really didn't hate me, but he was mad. Still is. He still tells us he hates it here and that he'd never make *his* kids move. His teacher is nice, and I've told her what's going on. And there's a group for new kids at his school that the guidance counselors run—he goes to that."

Jill was wise to accept professional help for her son. He needed someone in addition to his parents to help him work out his fury and sadness about feeling forced to move. His angry face may have kept other youngsters from approaching him when he needed some friendly gestures.

"I'll be really honest with you—I don't like it here at all," said sixteen-year-old Amy a year after her move. "My mom and dad know that. They've been great—like, my mom drives me and my friends back and forth from Maryland so we can see each other a lot. I don't like this town. There's no school spirit here. It's not like my old school—they have a lot of spirit. My teachers are OK—they make it easy to learn things. I'm getting better grades than I did in my old school. But I hate when teachers know you're new—they say, like, 'Why don't you stand up and introduce yourself.'"

"I've only got one friend here, another new girl. I told her about you interviewing me and she wants to talk to you. We really don't have much in common—I guess we're friends because we both hate it here. My real best friend is in Maryland—I get to call her when I want. I set the timer so the bill won't be too big."

"I stayed quiet when I came here—it didn't work for me. Other kids are really loud and friendly, but that wouldn't work for me either. Tell the kids who read your book to be themselves and try to make friends fast or else you'll be miserable and want to go back to your old home."

"I baby sit some. There are three families I sit for. It helps—I have something to do after school and weekends. Tell the parents who get your book to move kids at a younger age. Don't wait 'til kids are in junior high or high school. It's too late by then."

How did Amy's mother see it?

"Amy hates it here. I feel bad for her, she didn't want to move. She was so looking forward to graduating from her high school and she was really attached to the town and school and teachers and all her friends. I've told her that we have to stay here, and when she graduates she can go back to college and then live there. I had to say that because she kept telling me she wanted to go back—almost weekly she'd say she hates it here, she has no friends, she wants to go home. I mean weekly. I had to say, 'We're not moving back, we're here.'"

Amy's parents might have arranged for her to live with a friend while she finished school, and spend weekends with her family. But once the move was made, her mom was wise to hold firm. It could have made Amy uneasy to feel that her misery could force another upheaval on her family—too much power for a teen to handle. But, even though her grades were good, Amy's persistent anger, loneliness, and sadness signaled that she needed even more help than her concerned parents were providing.

There are a number of emotional states and behaviors that signal that youngsters are in distress. You may notice these in your own child.

PRE-SCHOOLERS:
- Disturbed sleep.
- Clinging/anxiety about separation from parents.
- Fears.
- Babyish behavior: loss of toilet training, baby talk or refusal to speak, asking to be dressed or fed, thumbsucking.
- Irritability.
- Passivity.

SCHOOL-AGE (INCLUDING TEENAGERS):
- Persistent shyness and isolation from others.
- Refusal to go to school.
- Trouble concentrating and finishing school work.
- Frequent bouts of tears and sadness.
- Low energy and loss of interest in activities or people that have usually been important.
- Feelings of hopelessness about the future, and any thought of suicide (whether spoken or written in a story).
- Stomachaches, headaches, or other unusual physical complaints.
- Disturbed sleep, with or without nightmares.
- Unexplained fears.
- Bedwetting.
- Loss of appetite or overeating.

- Nail biting, tooth grinding, hair pulling, and other habits that seem to express tension.
- Unusual crankiness and tendency to pick fights.
- Stealing.
- Frequent accidents.

As we've mentioned, most youngsters show signs of stress during the first weeks after a move. But if those signs persist, it's wise to talk them over with your child's health care provider, your child's teacher and guidance counselor, the school social worker or psychologist. Any of those professionals may encourage you to have your child evaluated by a mental health clinician, and help you locate the appropriate one.

Chapter 14 Exercises

We've described many ways that you can help your youngsters adjust to new homes, neighborhoods, schools, and communities. Here's a list of specific things to do:

- Spend time together looking at photographs of special people and places you've moved away from.
- If your budget allows it, let your youngsters phone friends and family members.
- If you can, arrange visits with your children's friends.
- Send letters and postcards.
- Ask teachers to write to your youngsters after you've moved.
- Make sure that your youngsters attend orientation sessions at their new schools. If you move after the new school year begins, ask the principal to arrange a tour for your youngster(s).
- Use 3"x5" index cards to help your children make personal identification cards to carry in their wallets, lunch boxes, or backpacks. ID cards will help them learn and remember your new address and phone number.
- Ask the school secretary for a copy of the school directory; encourage your youngsters to phone new friends.

- Find out what teachers at your youngsters' new schools do to make new students feel welcome. Let the teacher(s) know what your kid(s) might need in the first few days of school.
- Call the class parent(s) with any questions you have about the school or your new community.
- If your budget allows it, enroll your youngsters in some after school activities.
- Plant a garden—indoors or outside!
- Let your youngsters choose their bedrooms, and allow them to make a lot of decisions about how to decorate their rooms.
- Explore your new neighborhood together. Let each family member pick two or three places to check out, such as the public library, video rental store, playgrounds, sports facilities, and so forth.
- Put up a large-scale map of your new neighborhood and community. Every evening after dinner, talk together about what family members have learned about your new town, and add this information to the map.
- Arrange reliable (and fun) after-school care for younger children if you're not at home at the end of the school day.
- Let your youngster(s) know how to reach you during the day. If you're employed outside the home, encourage them to call you at your workplace when they get home from school.
- Plan some "down time" for your youngsters—time just to relax in your new home.
- Encourage your youngsters to tell you their feelings about all the changes in their lives following your move. Listen, and accept what you hear.
- Seek professional help if you think your youngster may need it.
- Encourage your teen to continue keeping a journal.

CHAPTER 15

Tending Your Love Relationships

PARTNERS MOVING TOGETHER

For couples, moving provides a special opportunity to learn new things about each other, about themselves, and about their relationship. But that learning depends on open and constructive communication and, unfortunately, communication often gets tangled in the stresses of the transition.

TANGLED COMMUNICATION

"I didn't want to leave Philadelphia—I've never been this far away from my family," Jill said, eighteen months after a move prompted by her husband losing his job and finding a new one in another state. "Now we live in a house that's smaller than what we had—I wish I could go home again. It's not that I don't like it here—I have friends here now, but it's not the same. I really resented that we had to move. I mean, I thought I'd spend my whole life in Philly."

"Now it's a lot better than it was the first couple of months. I didn't cry, but I was really depressed—I think I still am. People couldn't be nicer, so how come I'm still so mad about living here? Actually, I'm mad at my husband, but I can't tell him because he'd feel awful. Does that sound terrible? He knows it's his fault that we had to move, so I don't want to make him feel worse. I know it's hard for him, too. It wasn't his fault that he lost his job. He works really hard."

Like many movers who grieve over significant losses, Jill was angry at the person who had caused her pain—her husband. Yet, loving him and recognizing that the situation had been beyond his control, she criticized herself for her anger. Her sadness and longing for her birth family, her loss of self-respect because she was unhappy even though "people couldn't be nicer," and her self-reproach because she was so angry all interacted and spiraled her into depression.

Yet Jill wanted to protect her husband, especially from her anger. Many women share that wish, fearing that their anger is destructive, viewing their male partners as more brittle emotionally than they are themselves. But would Jill's struggle to conceal her anger have been constructive? Or even possible? Unless he was exclusively absorbed in his work, wouldn't Jill's husband have noticed signs of her unhappiness? Her anger may have leaked out in a stiffness of her body when they hugged, or an edge in her voice, or an irritable glance. Declaring her anger Off Limits could have set up a communication barrier between them.

We didn't find out what Jill's husband noticed about her misery. But we did hear how other men reacted to their wives.

"Looking back on our moves, what were the hardest things for you?" Kay asked Kurt, her husband. Supporting his career development, she had been the "following partner" through five moves, each causing the interruption of close, warm relationships with neighbors, friends, and relatives, as well as fragmentation of her own career. She was sad and increasingly resentful about those ruptures. Unlike Jean, she expressed her feelings openly.

"The hardest thing? Seeing how moving affects you," Kurt said. "How's that for honesty? When we move I have all the pressures of a new job and I'm kind of scared, and then I know that you're at home with the kids and I'm worried about how you're doing and how the kids are doing."

This was news to Kay—Kurt had never spoken of that worry. Through the moves, she had assumed that he viewed the children's well-being as her responsibility. She even felt that he had "dumped" that on her.

"It's hard to concentrate on my work when I'm worried that you're unhappy, you're lonely, and people sometimes aren't friendly. In our last move, that was a hard place to be new in."

"What about you? What was hard for you there?" asked Kay.

"Business school was worse than I expected. I was just a lowly student again, and that was tough after six years in management with the staff asking me about things. There I was, older than some of the faculty, but some of them treat you like an idiot."

Like many men in our competitive society, Kurt was sensitive to hierarchy. He had typical concerns about who is "one up" and who is "one down," who is respected and who is scorned. Losing his status as a manager must have shaken his self-esteem.

"I never thought about quitting, because I knew in the long run it was going to be good for all of us. But there were lots of days when I wondered how we'd make it. I had all those issues of my own to deal with at school, and then I'd come home and you'd be upset or angry about something, and I'd feel like I couldn't do much except hurry up and finish."

Kay's unhappiness made Kurt feel helpless. Since men typically try to deal with problems by taking action, his helpless position must have inflicted another bruise on his self-esteem

"What were some of the issues you can remember that I was dealing with?" Kay asked, wondering if Kurt had taken her needs seriously.

"You were really lonely, you missed your friends, we had no money, everyone around you was doing things that cost money and you couldn't do those things. All our moves meant that you had put your career aside, and I felt badly about that."

"Sometimes I felt guilty because I was the reason for the moving. Then sometimes I was angry because I was trying to tool up to provide for my family and it seemed so hard to juggle my marriage and my career. There were days when I'd think about how unhappy you were and my school performance was really affected—then I'd get angry because the problems were upsetting me so much at work."

Kurt was almost overwhelmed—guilty because he had caused the problems, helpless because he couldn't fix them. He worried about being an adequate provider, and felt anxious about his performance at school. If, after the upheaval of moving, he had failed in his studies, he would have felt deeply ashamed.

"I'd come home, and you'd be complaining about being lonely, or having to be with the kids all the time, or having no money."

"Do you know *now* that I wasn't complaining, that I was talking to you and that you sometimes were the only adult I had seen for two days?" Kay asked with an edge to her voice.

"Complaining" can be a demeaning word, close to "whining." Maybe Kurt chose it as a way of putting her down—retaliating against her because her "complaints" burdened him with feelings of helplessness and guilt.

In reacting to his term "complaining," Kay was showing that she did find it demeaning. She reached for reassurance that Kurt saw her as more than a complainer, and also that he understood her plight. She had needed to talk about her problems with someone she felt close to, and she had been cut off from her dearest friends.

"Yeah, now I know. You're talking, you're not complaining. Sometimes I forget that. I feel so guilty about all this and then I get defensive."

Kurt's comment, "sometimes I forget," hinted that he still had trouble appreciating Kay's need to talk about her distress. Maybe he wished she would take action to deal with her problems, rather than talking about them. He may have been a man who believed that venting emotions serves little purpose—one should either solve a problem or shrug it off. But he also reminded Kay that her distress stirred unbearable feelings in him, and that made it hard to listen..

Kurt had trouble listening, and trouble talking, too. His guilt about the pain caused by the move, as well as his resentment about Kay's reaction, got in the way of telling his wife that he was truly concerned about her.

Rather than feeling "dumped on," she might have felt supported if he had.

Kurt's words to Kay almost echoed Scott's words to Sylvia (Chapter 12). Powerful emotions had surged through both of these couples—resentment, anger, anxiety, and guilt. Both women expressed their feelings openly, both men closed themselves off, allowing their guilt and resentment to fester.

But there was also deep love and concern between the partners. Their intense conversations—each initiated by the woman—were much overdue, but at least they did happen.

Since both Kurt and Scott resented their partners' distress after their moves, it would be easy to conclude that Jill had made the wiser choice— keeping her anger to herself. But that seems unlikely. First, women who bottle up anger at a loved one, feeling guilty and ashamed because the anger seems unjustified, are candidates for psychological depression. Second, unless feelings are expressed, there is little possibility for mutual understanding and problem solving. Unhappy partners can stay isolated from each other in their private worlds of pain until negative feelings overshadow positive ones and their relationships unravel.

CONSTRUCTIVE COMMUNICATION

Hopefully, you'll safeguard your relationship from the beginning of your move. As a start, re-read RISKS TO YOUR LOVE PARTNERSHIP in Chapter 3. Then talk our ideas over together, identifying ways in which the stresses of moving are affecting you as a twosome. It's difficult to accept that a move—even a wanted move—can stir disagreeable feelings between loving partners. But accepting that fact puts you in the driver's seat. Rather than being driven by the emotions, you and your partner can be the drivers, actively planning your route through them.

It's hard to communicate troublesome emotions constructively. But try to consider WHEN and WHERE to communicate, as well as WHAT.

It's not easy to plan the WHEN. Emotions can burst out unexpectedly, taking you and your partner by surprise. But even if you find yourself "losing it," it's possible to turn the eruption into a useful communication. You might say something like this: "I'm really sorry I blew my stack. But the fact that I did tells me I need to talk with you about how sad/lonely/ hurt/mad I'm feeling. Could we find some time tonight/tomorrow/this weekend?" Involving your partner that way helps her or him feel like a collaborator rather than a victim. If one of you is "losing it" often, too much pressure is building up between conversations. You need to plan regular times together when you can each express your feelings in smaller, milder doses.

As you consider the WHERE, remember the differences in the ways in which men and women communicate (of course there are exceptions). Women, for example, often propose, "let's sit down and talk it over." They expect to face their partner as they talk. If the partner is a woman, that may be comfortable. But sitting face-to-face may be the last thing an action-oriented man wants.

How about a compromise? Could you take a walk together, releasing tension through the movement as you talk? Walking lets you be close without making either partner feel trapped. And walking allows you to look at each other some of the time, but also to avoid feeling your gazes are locked together. If you are not walkers, could you talk while you work in the garden, hang pictures together, wash the car, bundle the newspapers for recycling? Try to recall situations in which you and your partner have had effective communication in the past, and see if you can reproduce them now.

Gender differences also matter as you consider WHAT to communicate. Many men expect themselves to "fix" a problem that a woman brings up, so a woman might tell her male partner that she doesn't need or want a fix, but it would help her get a clearer perspective to talk things out. That lets him know that there's a useful role he can play, and his questions may help put the issues into focus. It also works well when the roles are reversed.

Some men feel impatient when women bring up emotions and issues they have discussed before. "We've already talked about this," he may object, causing her to feel put down. It helps if she can agree that she has brought the issue up before, and then point out that going over it again allows her to see it in a fresh light.

Men are often more reticent than women in talking about emotions. They may feel unsafe when they expose their "weak" or "soft" sides.

Anger is hard for both women and men to discuss. When you're angry, it's easy to launch an attack against your partner. Naturally, s/he becomes defensive, and probably angry in return. But there is a strategy that can make anger less of a tinderbox. Be mindful of the first pronoun you use when you begin talking. Rather than starting out "YOU" and then accusing and reproaching your partner for the behavior that has made you furious, why not start out with an "I"? "I'm angry because..." is often effective. You are accepting some responsibility for the troublesome emotion, rather than loading it onto your partner's shoulders.

Remember that anger is a response to a threat, and try to figure out in what way you have felt vulnerable or hurt. It's often easier and more useful to talk about the underlying threat than about the resulting anger. Here's an example: "When you were so late getting home from the office, I got scared that you might have slipped on the ice or had car trouble. Then when you breezed in and said you'd stopped for a beer with a colleague, it seemed really unfair. I'd been alone and scared that you were in trouble while you were having a great time. So I got mad." That approach might prompt your partner to say, "I can see that it really wasn't fair. Next time I'll be sure to call."

As you try to communicate honestly and constructively with each other, keep in mind that the circuits often become overloaded after a move. It may not be possible for both partners to stay open to distress signals from the other. For this reason, it is important to have more than one confidante. Until you develop trustworthy friendships in your new community, you may need to turn back—in visits, on the telephone, on electronic mail if you have access to it—to the people who were very close before your move

And what about non-verbal ways of soothing and supporting each other? Although we don't fully agree with the maxim that "actions speak louder than words," actions have their place. When Scott phoned Sylvia to come and see the blue scillas blooming by the church (Chapter 11), he was inviting her to share an exquisite sight as well as a happy memory. There are many such gestures that can convey how much you care about each other. What are your favorites—a back rub, a loaf of homemade bread, an evening of dancing? Call them to mind and use them!

Finally, try to monitor each other's emotional well-being, as well as your own. Both grief and depression are common among movers, but they are not the same. Grief, kindled by loss of loved people, places, or objects, is a state of sadness and longing. Depression, kindled by an experience of failure and perhaps by a biological vulnerability, is a state of hopelessness, helplessness, loss of interest, energy, and self-esteem. Sleep, appetite, sexual drive, and—in women—the menstrual cycle are often affected. Sometimes the depression is masked with alcohol, binge eating, overbuying, or other excesses. Often it lurks behind physical ailments or unusual irritability.

Depression may lift spontaneously. A mover may experience blue days, or even weeks, with periods of well-being in between. But it may also deepen until the individual is unable to function at work or respond appropriately to family members. In whatever way it is expressed, depression can take a serious toll on the affected person and on loved ones also. Severe depression can lead to suicide.

If you suspect that you or your partner are sliding into a persistent depression, it's important to seek out a professional evaluation. Start with your primary physician, or turn to the mental health center in your community for a referral to a well trained clinical social worker, psychologist, psychiatrist, or pastoral counselor. The combination of psychological counseling and a well chosen anti-depressant medication can be marvelously effective.

COUPLES WHO ARE SEPARATED

Although most couples prefer to move together, that may not happen. One may want to accept a job before the other can locate work in his or her field. One may want to stay behind to finish college or professional training, or to wind up a business, or to fulfill obligations to family members. One may need to go ahead to locate housing; one may need to stay behind to dispose of housing.

Couples with children may decide to divide the family so that a youngster can finish school. Or it may work best for one parent to spend a last summer with the children in familiar activities and among close friends.

If both partners have supportive neighbors, friends, or colleagues, the interlude can be pleasant. In fact, each one may develop or rediscover competence in spheres usually handled by the other—what to do when the car won't start, or how to cook a palatable meal. Each one may develop or rediscover interests not shared by the other, and spend free time in art galleries or learning to ski.

But there will be a shadow side, too. Both partners are likely to miss each other, sometimes painfully, and to have lonely, sad, and anxious moments. Sleep may not come easily without the warm closeness of a partner in bed. There will be nobody right there to hear about the day's satisfactions and disappointments, or to share a glorious sunset.

Most adults keep on growing and developing through their lives. When you live together, you probably notice changes in each other and try to accommodate to them. When you've been separated, you may find that each one has grown in a different direction, or is growing at a different pace.

There may be a twinge of alienation during a visit. For example, you may have become a creative cook, and feel affronted when your partner expects to take over the kitchen the way s/he used to do. You may have started jogging at sunrise, and your partner may expect to make love when you first waken, as you used to do. You may have been in sole charge of the children, and find it hard to share decisions and authority for a weekend.

People in your community—especially very traditional ones—may raise their eyebrows about your separation. Some will suppose that there's trouble in your relationship. Some will be critical of your decision. And a woman on her own is still apt to have a harder time than a man. There are vestigial beliefs that a solitary woman is a predator, ready to lure someone else's man. Those ideas cause women to be excluded from social doings among couples, whereas an unattached man is often welcome. Too, an unattached man is often viewed as appealingly helpless in the domestic sphere, and needing to be taken in for a meal.

There may be a disparity in the experience of each partner, and that can breed troubled feelings. One partner may be exhilarated by new work while the stay-behind regretfully winds down a satisfying project. Or one may feel warmly tended while the other feels coldly neglected.

When Kurt moved in advance of Kay to start business school, he was painfully lonely. Not only had he lost the collegial recognition and respect he was used to, but also the enthusiastic welcome of his wife and children at the end of each day. Kay, in contrast, was nurtured by close friends and relatives while she readied the household for moving.

It would be hard for a partner in Kurt's position not to be envious and resentful.

There are risks involved in moving separately. But if you allow yourselves to face them, and actively plan for the interlude of separation, the risks can be minimized.

HELPFUL STRATEGIES

You can't find solutions until you've identified the problems. So it's helpful for each partner to identify what s/he hopes for, worries about, and fears during the forthcoming separation. On the sunny side, separation may offer freedoms and opportunities. It's tricky to let your partner know that you're glad that s/he'll be away. It may work best to frame it as a reassurance: "I think I'll get on all right because I'll take time to go to the museums that bore you."

On the shadow side, you may fear that your partner will find that your relationship is less important than s/he thought, or that s/he will be attracted to someone else. That's tricky to communicate too, without casting aspersions on your partner's loyalty. But it can be done if you take responsibility for the fear: "I seem to be feeling insecure, and I'll need extra reassurance about how much we care about each other."

In fact, as you each identify a worry or fear, try to let your partner know what could be helpful in assuaging the concern. You may need to brainstorm the problem together.

Do you know people who have been separated from each other because of external circumstances (not because their relationship failed)? Ask them to share their experience. What was helpful, what was not helpful, what would they do differently another time?

Identify people who might be helpful during your separation: friends, neighbors, relatives, colleagues, baby-sitters, clergy, health professionals. Let them know about the forthcoming separation and what kinds of help you may need.

People who want to be supportive may make specific offers: "I'm going to the store—what do you need?" or "I'd like to baby-sit for you one night this week. Which night would you like?"

Others may be just as well meaning, but make vague offers: "Call if you need anything." You'll need to be specific: "Could we go out to dinner together?" or "I need bread—can you pick some up on the way over?"

Try to accept help that is offered. That doesn't mean agreeing with a suggestion that wouldn't meet your needs (inappropriate offers can usually be transformed if you express appreciation and then make an alternative suggestion). It does mean that this is no time to be stoical, trying to prove your competence and independence. If you allow yourself to be over-stretched, both you and your relationship will suffer.

Involve your partner in developing a communication strategy including WHEN, WHERE, AND WHAT. First, talk over what each of you hopes for in the way of letters and phone calls. How often would you want them, and at what times of day or evening (you may need to change that after the separation has occurred and new schedules are in place)? Will it work best to call spontaneously, or to agree to take turns?

A plan for visits has to take into account schedules, travel time, and finances. It also should take into account psychological need. One partner may like to do things on the spur of the moment. The other may need the comfort of looking forward to definite dates. That needs negotiation.

There will be moments when one or the other, or both of you, are resentful, angry, frustrated, sad, and lonely—either about the separation or about events in your daily life. It's a challenge to work out a strategy for communicating troubled feelings, and planning a strategy is easier than carrying it out. But it's worth a try.

Could you make a pact to start every phone conversation or visit with the positive experiences you've had, and then move on to the problems? Or would it work better to get the negatives out of the way, and then enjoy the positives before you have to hang up? Or start and end with positives, with the problems sandwiched in the middle like peanut butter? You might get clues if you consider how each of you handles your chores and pleasures in daily living. Does it feel good to get the chores out of the way and then reward yourself with the fun? Or do you like to stoke your furnace with pleasure before you tackle the dreary tasks? You may each have different preferences, and need to agree to take turns in modes of communication. Be mindful that if your strategy breaks down—it probably will at times—just planning it together increases your understanding of each other.

If one of you will be a single parent during the separation, remember the oxygen mask (Chapter 9). Before your partner leaves, think together about ways you can nurture yourself as you carry that heavy responsibility.

Nurture each other with a Survival Kit, prepared before the separation. This could be a basket of items that each will enjoy during the separation—favorite coffees or teas, candies, books, tickets to a play or concert, photographs, and tapes of each other's voices (it's usually easier for people to recall the way a loved one looks than the way s/he sounds). If you'll be visiting each other, the Survival Boxes can be refilled.

Finally, be mindful that separations in the present can revive sadness and anxiety connected with separations in the past. Naturally, if your partner is really unsafe—in military action, for example—you'll probably be worried and frightened most of the time. But if you are both safe, well housed, well fed, and with some friendly people available, and yet one of you feels persistent dread, fear, and sadness, that may signal that an overwhelming experience from the past is being stirred up again. Consider talking it over with a mental health clinician.

Tending Your Love Relationships 237

We have described many ways in which moving challenges men and women, and strains the love bonds between them. If the strains are unrecognized or neglected, the bonds can unravel. Yet that doesn't have to happen. In fact, the opposite can be true.

Your move provides you with a special opportunity to take a fresh look, a deep look, a broad look at your lives as individuals, as well as your life as a couple. It can spur you to think about your capabilities and your limitations, your hopes and your fears, your dreams and your disappointments.

An understanding of the complex tasks of moving, and the powerful emotions they arouse, can foster constructive communication. The resources of two minds can be pooled to solve new problems. But just as important, your relationship can become more trusting, more empathic, more resilient. Each accepting your right to receive care and your responsibility to give care, you can develop a relationship that we hope will become the model for the 21st century—a relationship of mutual concern, a relationship of true interdependence.

Chapter 15 Exercises

EXERCISE A

If you're moving with a partner, here are some issues to think about and talk over together:

So far, our move has been positive for me because

_____

_____

So far, our move has been difficult for me because

_____

_____

When I think about what our move is like for you, it seems that you're enjoying

_____

_____

When I think again about what our move is like for you, it seems that you're finding it difficult to

_____

_____

During the next few days/weeks I'll need

_____

_____

What are some things that you'll need in the next few days/weeks?

_____

_____

EXERCISE B

If your move involves separation from your partner, talk over these hopes and wishes together:

While we're apart I'd like you to

_____

_____

_____

While we're apart I'd like you *not* to

_____

_____

_____

What are some things that you'd like me to do while we're apart?

_____

_____

_____

What are some things that you'd like me *not* to do while we're apart?

_____

_____

_____

When we visit I'd like to

_____

_____

_____

When we visit I *don't* want to

_____

_____

_____

What are some things you'd like me to do when we visit?

_____

_____

_____

What are some things you'd like *not* to do when we visit?

_____

_____

_____

When our separation is over I'd like to

_____

_____

_____

When our separation is over I *don't* want to

_____

_____

_____

What else would you like to tell me about our separation?

_____

_____

_____

EXERCISE C

You'll need your journal for this exercise. Each day, write about what you did to take care of your partner and what your partner did to take care of you.

SUGGESTED READING FOR CHILDREN

We have grouped some helpful books by the age level of the reader. Some of the books may be out of print. Ask your librarian to help you find those through an inter-library loan.

PRE-SCHOOL CHILDREN
(to be read with an adult)

Hughes, Shirley. *Moving Molly.* Englewoode Cliffs, NJ: Prentice-Hall, Inc., 1979

Johnston, Tony. *The Quilt Story.* New York: G.P. Putnam's Sons, 1985.

Keats, Ezra Jack. *The Trip.* New York: Greenwillow Books, 1978.

O'Donnell, Elizabeth Lee. *Maggie Doesn't Want to Move.* New York: Four Winds Press, 1987.

Rogers, Fred. *Moving.* New York: G.P. Putnam's Sons, 1987.

Sharmat, Marjorie Weinman. *Gila Monsters Meet You at the Airport.* New York: MacMillan Pub. Co., 1980.

Watson, Wendy. *Moving.* New York: Thomas Y. Crowell Co., 1978.

Zolotow, Charlotte. *Janey.* New York: Harper and Row, 1973.

SCHOOL-AGE CHILDREN

Barger, Gary. *Life. Is. Not. Fair.* New York: Clarion Books, 1984 (Grades 6-9)

Bottner, Barbara. *The World's Greatest Expert on Absolutely Everything Is Crying.* New York: Harper and Row, 1984 (Grades 3-6).

Cannon, A.E. *Amazing Gracie.* New York: Delacorte Press, 1991 (Grades 6-9)

Carrick, Carol. *What A Wimp!* New York: Clarion Books, 1983 (Grades 4-6)

Cheatham, K. Follis. *The Best Way Out.* New York: Harcourt, Brace, Janovich, 1982 (Grades 6-8).

Park, B. *The Kid in the Red Jacket.* New York: Alfred A. Knopf Inc., 1987 (Grades 4-6).

HELPFUL RESOURCES FOR ADULTS

BOOKS

Bastress, Frances. *The New Relocating Spouse's Guide to Employment: Options and Strategies in the US and Abroad.* Manassas Park, VA: Impact Publications, 1993.

Harrison, Charles Hampton, 2nd ed. *Public Schools USA: Comparative Guide to School Districts.* Princeton, NJ: Peterson's Guides, Inc.,1991.

McCollum, Audrey. *The Trauma of Moving: Psychological Issues for Women.* Newbury Park, CA: Sage Publications, Inc., 1990.

Peterson's Independent Secondary Schools, 1991-92. Princeton, NJ: Peterson's Guides, Inc., 1991.

Rosenberg, Lee and Rosenberg, SaraLee H. *50 Fabulous Places to Raise Your Family.* Hawthorne, NJ: Career Press, 1993.

Rosenberg, Lee and Rosenberg, SaraLee. *50 Fabulous Places to Retire in America.* Hawthorne, NJ: Career Press, 1991.

Toomey, Priscilla R. *20 Week Guide To Your Best Move.* A practical guide to selling your home, locating and financing a new one, and moving your household. Available through MovePower, 1117 East Putnam Ave., #170, Riverside, CT 06878. Tel. 800-692-3786.

World Chamber of Commerce Directory. Washington, DC: U.S. Chamber of Commerce, 1994.

ORGANIZATIONS

American Association of Retired
Persons
601 E St. NW
Washington, DC 20049
Tel. 202-434-2277

American Association of University
Women
1111 16th St. NW
Washington, DC 20036
Tel. 202-785-7700

Council for Exceptional Children
1920 Association Drive
Reston, VA 22091
Tel. 703-620-3660

Institute for Retired Professionals
New School for Social Research
66 West 12th St.
New York, NY 10011
Tel. 212-229-5683

Mothers at Home
8310-A Old Courthouse Rd.
Vienna, VA 22182
Tel. 703-827-5903

National Association of Child Care
Resources and Referral Agencies
1319 F St. NW, Suite 606
Washington, DC 20004
Tel. 202-393-5501

National Association for Gifted
Children
1155 15th St. NW, No. 1002
Washington, DC 20005
Tel. 202-785-4268

National Assocation Of Mothers'
Centers
336 Fulton Ave.
Hempstead, NY 11550
Tel. 516-486-6614 or 800-645-3828

National Center For Learning
Disabilities
99 Park Ave.
New York, NY 10016
Tel. 212-687-7211

National Homeschool Association
PO Box 290
Hartland, MI 48353-0290
Tel. 513-772-9580

National Information Center For
Children And Youth With
Disabilities
PO Box 1492
Washington, DC 20013
Tel. 703-893-6061 or 800-999-5599

National Organization On Disability
910 16TH St. NW, Suite 600
Washington, DC 20006
Tel. 202-229-1187 or 800-248-2253

National Parent Network On
Disabilities
1600 Prince St., Suite 115
Alexandra, VA 22314
Tel. 703-684-6763

Network For Professional Women
216 Main St.
Hartford, CT 06103
Tel. 203-727-1988

Retired and Senior Volunteer Program
1100 Vermont Avenue NW
Washington, DC 20525
Tel. 202-606-5000

Women Work! The National Network
For Women's Employment
1625 K St. NW, Suite 300
Washington, DC 20006
Tel. 202-467-6346 or 800-235-2732